GLASGOW 1900

Van Gogh Museum
Amsterdam
The Netherlands

20 November 1992 - 7 February 1993

Cover
John Lavery, *A Rally*, 1885
(cat. 34; detail)

GLASGOW 1900 ART & DESIGN

Elizabeth Cumming

Waanders Publishers, Zwolle
Van Gogh Museum, Amsterdam

Contents

Preface

Glasgow 1900 has been put together as a reciprocal exhibition for *The Age of Van Gogh* which was shown at the Burrell Collection as the fitting climax to the visual arts programme of Glasgow's year as European City of Culture in 1990. Glasgow Museums and Art Galleries and the Van Gogh Museum are delighted to be working together again on our second collaborative venture.

This is the first in-depth exploration of art and design in Glasgow around 1900, and will be seen only in Amsterdam. It shows that Glasgow was no aesthetic backwater, but a European city at the forefront of cultural developments and achievements. Designers, artists, dealers, collectors, educators - particularly those at the School of Art - all contributed to this remarkable flowering of art and design in Glasgow in the period c. 1880-1914.

The exhibition has been selected almost entirely from the collections of Glasgow Museums and Art Galleries by guest curator Dr Elizabeth Cumming in close cooperation with Stefan van Raay, Head of Exhibitions at the Van Gogh Museum. Dr Cumming edited the catalogue and contributed two introductory essays. A third essay has been written by Roger Billcliffe, while individual entries and data for biographical notes have been prepared by staff members of Glasgow Museums and Art Galleries, Elizabeth Arthur, Celine Blair, Brian Blench, Patricia Collins and Daniel Robbins. We are grateful to all the contributors, to Dr Murray Simpson and Dr Andrew McCormick for copy editing and Moira McKendry for able secretarial assistance. The exhibition has been coordinated in Glasgow by Hugh Stevenson and in Amsterdam by Aly Noordermeer. Julian Andrews, director of the British Council in Amsterdam, has been instrumental in the close cooperation of both museums. The Council in particular assisted with the organisation of the symposium on Charles Rennie Mackintosh to be held in Amsterdam.

We also wish to thank the Hunterian Art Gallery, University of Glasgow, Mackintosh Collection, the Glasgow School of Art and Edinburgh City Museums and Art Galleries for agreeing to lend works to the exhibition at the Van Gogh Museum, and to the Hunterian Art Gallery for permission to quote from the papers of Charles Rennie Mackintosh.

A selection from the exhibition will be shown at Glasgow Art Gallery and Museum later in 1993.

Ronald de Leeuw
Director
Van Gogh Museum

Julian Spalding
Director
Glasgow Museums and Art Galleries

Abbre-viations

The following abbreviations have been used in the catalogue:

ACGB
Arts Council of Great Britain

ARA
Associate of the Royal Academy

Billcliffe, *The Glasgow Boys*
Roger Billcliffe, *The Glasgow Boys,* London 1990

Billcliffe, *Mackintosh Watercolours*
Roger Billcliffe, *Mackintosh Watercolours,* London 1978

Billcliffe, *Mackintosh Textile Designs*
Roger Billcliffe, *Mackintosh Textile Designs,* London 1982

Billcliffe, *Mackintosh Furniture and Interiors*
Roger Billcliffe, *Charles Rennie Mackintosh: The Complete Furniture, Furniture Designs and Interiors,* London 1986

Burkhauser, *Glasgow Girls*
Jude Burkhauser (ed.), *Glasgow Girls: Women in Art and Design 1880-1920,* Edinburgh 1990

cat.
catalogue number(s)

CEMA
Council for the Encouragement of Music and the Arts

GAGM
Glasgow Art Gallery and Museums

GIFA
Glasgow Institute of the Fine Arts

GMAG
Glasgow Museums and Art Galleries

1980 Glasgow
Exhibition *Glasgow School of Art Embroidery 1894-1920,* Glasgow Museums and Art Galleries 1980

1982 Glasgow
Centenary Exhibition of the Glasgow Society of Lady Artists, Collins Art Gallery, University of Strathclyde 1982

1984 Glasgow
Exhibition *The Glasgow Style 1890-1920,* Glasgow Museums and Art Galleries 1984

1990 Glasgow
Jude Burkhauser (curator), exhibition *Glasgow Girls: Women in Art and Design 1880-1920,* Glasgow Museums and Art Galleries 1990

1968 Glasgow Boys
The Glasgow Boys, Scottish Arts Council touring exhibition, 1968-69

illus.
illustration

NA-CF
National Art - Collections Fund

NEAC
New English Art Club

PRSA
President of the Royal Scottish Academy

PRSW
President of the Royal Scottish Society of Painters in Watercolours

RA
Royal Academy, Royal Academician

RGIFA
Royal Glasgow Institute of the Fine Arts

repr.
reprinted

RSA
Royal Scottish Academy, Royal Scottish Academician

RSW
Member of the Royal Scottish Society of Painters in Watercolours

Reekie, *Margaret Macdonald Mackintosh*
Pamela Reekie, *Margaret Macdonald Mackintosh,* Glasgow (Hunterian Art Gallery), 1983

Robertson, *Mackintosh at the Hunterian*
Pamela Robertson, *Charles Rennie Mackintosh at the Hunterian Art Gallery,* Glasgow (Hunterian Art Gallery) 1991

SAC
Scottish Arts Council

SSA
Society of Scottish Artists

1902 Turin
The Turin International Exhibition of Decorative Art, 1902

1983 Turin
Exhibition *Glasgow Style,* Galleria Felice Casorati, Turin 1983

Industry
and art

Elizabeth Cumming

There are many reasons why the visual arts flowered in Glasgow between 1880 and 1914, the years covered by the present exhibition. This could not have occurred, however, without the expansion of trade and industry and the consequent accumulation of private wealth in the mid-nineteenth century. By 1900 Glasgow richly deserved its reputation as the 'Second City of the British Empire' and the 'Sixth City of Europe'.

The florescence of Glasgow occurred long after the dawn of the Industrial Revolution. The population more than trebled in the sixty years between 1840 and 1900, rising from just under three hundred thousand to nearly a million. This dramatic demographic expansion went hand in hand with the intense industrial urbanisation that was even more acute in Scotland than in the rest of the British Isles. One twentieth of the Scottish population lived in Glasgow in 1800, as compared to one fifth a century later.

Around the turn of the century the city's wealth was generated by four main industries - shipbuilding, engineering, textiles and whisky - and by every conceivable type of trade. But Glasgow was no longer only the manufacturing centre of the west of Scotland and, in the case of heavy engineering and shipbuilding, the British Empire: it had also become an international marketplace.

In the beginning, Glasgow's industrial production had been based on grain. Eighteenth-century mills still stand on the banks of the rivers Cart and Kelvin. Bread and biscuit production, as opposed to grinding grain, became a lucrative industry in the late nineteenth century, and remained such until World War Two. But the textile industry was the city's first great success, for their early contributions to which two Glasgow merchants, James Finlay and David Dale, are remembered. Together with Robert Owen, Dale established the community of New Lanark southeast of Glasgow for textile workers in the early nineteenth century. Cotton was normally spun in the countryside, but with the introduction of power looms in the 1820s, industrial production came to be increasingly concentrated in the cities; many of the factories were located in the area west of the Cathedral now known as Merchant City. After Glasgow's share of the tobacco and sugar trade had been usurped by the fledgling United States, from the 1830s cotton and its associated chemical industries became the principal source of employment. In the late nineteenth century carpet-weaving emerged, dominated by the firms of Templeton and Lyle. As in the case of the cotton industry, carpet-weavers relied on smaller, auxiliary industries to do the dyeing, printing and bleaching. In time more firms sprang up to serve the various facets of Glasgow's industrial complex. Most paint works, for example, were founded in order to supply shipbuilders.

Technology kept pace with the industrial growth of the city: just as mechanical engineering had developed to meet the needs of the grain and textile mills, so the other industries stimulated progress in the field of nautical engineering. A famous example is the mill engine used to propel Henry Bell's ship *Comet* in 1812, thus triggering the invention and manufacture of marine engines.

By the dawn of the Victorian age the city was ideally positioned for industrial expansion, at the hub of a canal system for transporting iron, timber, stone and, last but not least, coal. The advent of the railroad further expedited transport within the region and beyond, besides creating still more jobs. To the south and east lay rich coal and iron deposits, the cornerstone of Victorian Glasgow's wealth. To the west the river Clyde retained its commercial utility; along its banks shipyards and docks sprang up over the next half century. Iron ships were built from the late 1830s, but as land values rose, the shipyards were forced to move down river. Ship and locomotive building formed the backbone of the city's new heavy industry, which led to the local manufacture of rivets, bolts, nuts, boilers, cranes, pumps and so forth.

The character of Scotland's capital, Edinburgh, was very different indeed. Situated some forty-five miles to the east, it remained the heart of the country's legal and banking systems and seat of the established Church. Throughout the nineteenth century Edinburgh's largely service-oriented economy was run by professionals, merchants and artisans. Though no Scottish parliament had convened in the capital since 1707, the city seemed content with its role within Scotland and had little inclination to industrialise further.

Between approximately 1780 and 1830 the first phase of Edinburgh's New Town was completed, heralding more blatant segregation between the professional and working classes. Then between 1830 and 1875 a business centre was created along the main thoroughfare of the New Town, namely Princes Street. Glasgow underwent similar changes: merchants moved into new houses in the West End, where a shopping and business centre developed around Buchanan Street, while the old heart of Glasgow sank into disrepair. The working classes were packed into tenements. By the middle of the century the historic districts of both cities were derelict.

In the 1840s the new railroad companies partly cleared the slums of Glasgow and Edinburgh. In Glasgow, the Corporation (as the city council was called) did its utmost to improve the appalling conditions, but the sheer scale of the problem defied a complete solution. With the passage of the City Improvement Act of 1866, hygiene and fresh air became top priorities for all social classes: new water and gas systems were installed, public laundries and hospitals built and parks laid out. Private

1.1 *Jozef Israëls, The Frugal Meal, c. 1870-75 (Glasgow Museums and Art Galleries) cat. 4*

development accompanied these municipal improvements as public houses, theatres, factories and warehouses were constructed, and middle-class housing sprang up to the west and south of the centre. For many the quality of life improved dramatically and despite the persistent problem of the slums Glaswegians had much to be proud of. The city's new self-awareness as an industrial centre was evinced by one building in particular: the City Chambers in George Square, built between 1882 and 1890. The building - a 'free and dignified treatment of the Italian Renaissance' according to the architect William Young (1843-1900) - symbolised mercantile prosperity.[1]

The wealth of the new industrialists was enhanced to no small degree by government legislation and generous tax laws. Income tax was low, and company profits were not taxed at all. The mercantile middle class had both disposable income and the leisure to enjoy it. The railway system enabled the captains of business and industry to have a house in town and one in the country, usually north or northwest of the city. Then as now such individuals invested in pictures for prestige and profit. In the third quarter of the nineteenth century Northern European art held the greatest appeal, especially the paintings of the Barbizon and Hague Schools. The scenes of everyday life among the lower classes by such masters as Jozef Israëls (fig. 1.1), Anton Mauve, Bernard Blommers, the Maris brothers and, to a lesser extent, Millet mirrored a vanishing way of life in rural Scotland that appealed to Glasgow's *nouveaux riches*. These pictures also looked well alongside those produced by members of the recently established Scottish school of painting. Just as the genre work of Scottish artists from David Wilkie to the Faeds had appealed to upper-class collectors of the previous generation, so contemporary Dutch and French painting attracted the new collectors. Neither the Dutch nor the Scottish pictures were overtly political; rather, they conveyed a typically Protestant sense of frugality.[2] The artists depicted everyday scenes of contented if impoverished peasants who eked out a living from the land, and thus met the growing demand for anecdotal painting. The affluent middle class bought Hague School paintings to display their wealth and boldly to express their new

rank within British society.

The presence of Dutch and French pictures at international exhibitions in London, Manchester and Edinburgh in the 1860s, 1870s and 1880s helped expose this new audience to recent European art. Though large-scale, popular exhibitions continued to stimulate international rivalry in design and manufacture and brought the worlds of trade and art together, the years 1880 to 1914 also witnessed the dramatic growth of the art trade. As demand for paintings burgeoned - and the number of professional artists correspondingly increased - so the gallery-based art market quickly expanded. By the turn of the century the fine art trade included prints, interior decoration and antiques as well as paintings and sculpture. The Glasgow art market peaked between 1895 and 1905, during which period the number of professional dealers increased eightfold, from four to over thirty.

In the 1880s, work by members of the Barbizon and Hague Schools could be seen in the Glasgow galleries of dealers such as Craibe Angus (1830-1899), whose business, which opened at 159 Queen Street in 1874, was by now well established. Of the older Glasgow dealers Angus was one of the most interesting, yet surprisingly little is known about him, apart from the fact that he was personally connected with Holland. Through the Scots-born dealer and stained-glass artist Daniel Cottier (1839-1891) he met the Dutch dealer Elbert Jan van Wisselingh (d. 1912), Cottier's London manager, who married one of Angus's daughters in 1887. Therefore it is not surprising that Craibe Angus was responsible for cultivating a taste for modern Dutch masters in Glasgow; his influence is particularly evident in James Donald's collection, which was lent to the 1888 Glasgow International Exhibition and then bequeathed to the city in 1905.

Fortunately we know a bit more about a dealer of a subsequent generation whose impact on Glasgow art and taste was tremendous. The Glaswegian collector William Burrell wrote that Alexander Reid (1854-1928) had done more than anyone else

to introduce fine pictures to Scotland and to create a love of art. He had a marvellous flair for French 19th Century ... and was looked up to by the Paris dealers with the greatest respect.[3]

With Reid, the international art trade reached new heights. He was doubtless partly responsible for the early twentieth-century appetite for more avant-garde art. The son of James G. Reid, who founded the Glasgow firm of carvers and gilders, Kay and Reid, in 1857, was sent to Paris in 1887 to work for the dealers Boussod & Valadon. While in the French capital he is said to have lodged with Theo van Gogh, brother of Vincent and manager of one of the firm's branches.[4] Vincent van Gogh painted two portraits of

1.2 Vincent van Gogh,
Portrait of Alexander Reid, *1887*
(Glasgow Museums and Art
Galleries) cat. 8

Reid, who was in fact the artist's only British sitter. In 1888 Reid returned with one of the portraits to Glasgow (fig. 1.2), where in March 1889 he opened a gallery - *La Société des Beaux-Arts* - at 232 West George Street, before moving into larger premises at 124 St Vincent Street in 1894 and, in 1904, to West George Street. His gallery remained in business until 1931, though Reid himself retired in 1926, at which point the gallery was taken over by the London dealer Lefèvre.

There were few serious collectors in Glasgow who did not buy from Reid. Famed for showing works by Sisley, Monet, Pissarro (cat. 6) and Degas in Glasgow, he also dealt in a number of other schools and periods. Though he specialised in French and Dutch pictures he also championed contemporary Scottish artists, including the Glasgow School, many of whom became personal friends. Reid bought as well as sold, and frequently acted as an intermediary between Glasgow collectors.

Some of the finest pictures sold by these dealers to such local industrialists as W.A. Coats, Leonard Gow and William Burrell were subsequently bequeathed to the city. Indeed, in Glasgow (as generally in other cities in both Britain and Holland) a number of donations and bequests formed the basis of the municipal art collection. Only in the early twentieth century did Glasgow Corporation begin to extend their art and museum collections through purchase. On the basis of such bequests one can chart the history of artistic taste in the west of Scotland.

The bequest of Archibald McLellan (1797-1854) - a wealthy coach-builder and deacon-convener (or chairman) of the Trades House, a chamber of commerce and manufacture - formed the nucleus of Glasgow's art collection. McLellan also gave the city a building in Sauchiehall Street in which to display his donation. He died insolvent, however, and the Corporation was forced to pay his creditors. In effect the collection was purchased for £15,000 and the Sauchiehall Street property for £29,000. McLellan had bought much of the collection, including many works by Old Masters of the Italian, Dutch and Flemish Schools, some thirty years before. His taste in pictures was typical of the age and predated the vogue for French painting; indeed, of the 427 items in the catalogue published in 1855, only thirty-six were French. In the mid 1870s McLellan's collection was augmented by the bequest of William Euing (1788-1874), a marine insurance underwriter; it comprised one hundred paintings, again mostly Dutch and Flemish.

Though other bequests followed, the finest pictures Glasgow acquired in the late nineteenth century derived from the collection of James Reid of Auchterarder (1823-1894), chief director and sole partner of Neilson, Reid & Co., Hydepark Locomotive Works in Glasgow, which claimed to be the largest locomotive manufacturers in Europe.

Reid's sons donated only ten French and British paintings from the collection, but these included a masterpiece by Corot entitled *Souvenir d'Italie.*

McLellan, Euing and Reid of Auchterarder (cat. 7) had set a precedent in Glasgow. Two chemical manufacturers, James Donald (1830-1905) and William Chrystal (1854-1921), left paintings and drawings to the city (fig. 1.3). Donald, a partner in the firm of George Miller & Co., had been a client of Craibe Angus and lent some of his French pictures to the 1888 Glasgow International Exhibition. With his bequest the city acquired its first important examples of the Barbizon School, including two important pictures by Millet, namely the oil *Going to Work* (cat. 5) and the pastel *The Sheepfold.* Donald also bequeathed a number of Dutch paintings and drawings from the seventeenth and nineteenth centuries, which included work by Kalf, Blommers and Bosboom. William Chrystal left ten French and British paintings by artists such as Lhermitte, Monticelli, Fantin-Latour and Daubigny, which were only received seventeen years after his death, in 1938.

If taste did not change dramatically after 1890, at least it broadened. William Allen Coats (1853-1926), partner in the Paisley thread manufacturing firm of J. & P. Coats, is now remembered as a collector for having purchased Vermeer's *Christ in the House of Martha and Mary* (National Gallery of Scotland, Edinburgh). From Alexander Reid he bought Hague and Barbizon School pictures, and paintings by Boudin, Monticelli, Géricault, Jongkind, Bosboom and, last but not least, the contemporary artist Joseph Crawhall, whose sophisticated work - along with that of John Lavery - may have had more appeal than any of the other so-called Glasgow Boys.[5]

Another important collector during this period was Thomas Glen Arthur (1857-1907) of the firm Messrs Arthur and Co. - 'at the head of the Scottish trade in Textile Manufacturers and all allied departments' - who purchased Degas and Courbet as well as Boudin, Fantin-Latour, Bosboom, Matthijs Maris and Whistler from Reid and Craibe Angus.[6]

1.3 Jean Baptiste Camille Corot, The Woodcutter, *1865-70 (Glasgow Museums and Art Galleries) cat. 3*

1.4 Matthijs Maris, Butterflies, c. 1900 (Glasgow Museums and Art Galleries, the Burrell Collection). Purchased by William Burrell in 1901.

Reid may have been the only dealer in Britain in the 1890s with direct access to many artists in Paris, including Degas. Arthur Kay (c. 1862-1939), also a partner in Messrs Arthur and Co., bought the occasional modern piece, such as Manet's *Café, Place du Théâtre Français* (now in the Burrell Collection), but generally preferred the Old Masters, including Rembrandt and Saenredam; his memoirs, *Treasure Trove in Art* (1939), betray more than a hint of snobbishness. But, as Richard Marks has pointed out, these Scottish collectors were the first in Britain to buy Manet and Degas.[7] Reid mounted an exhibition of Degas, Monticelli, Pissarro and Sisley in London in December 1891 which then travelled to Glasgow two months later along with still other pictures; it was from this exhibition that Kay purchased Degas's *L'Absinthe.*[8]

The collection of art and antiquities formed by William Burrell (1861-1958) is world famous. Its fascinating history serves to illustrate the development of this collector's idiosyncratic taste. Burrell was a partner in his father's Glasgow-based shipowning firm called Burrell and Son. Collecting was virtually a second career for him, and combined the excitement of the chase with the more domestic pleasure of furnishing his house. Though he only became a really great collector after the First World War, with the help of a number of distinguished scholars, the ready availability of outstanding Dutch and French pictures in Glasgow by the 1890s enabled him to make important acquisitions right from the start.

The growth of Burrell's collection is most fully documented from 1911, when he began to formalise his acquisition policy by keeping account books. He had started buying art cautiously twenty years before. From notes preserved at Glasgow Museums and Art Galleries, it seems his earliest purchases were relatively conservative: Dutch seventeenth-century portraits of children, which he bought in Holland like souvenirs, as it were. In the late 1890s Burrell's interests extended to the decorative arts, and he returned to the Low Countries on several occasions to buy tapestries, furniture and *objets d'art* under the guidance of his friend, the Edinburgh architect Robert Lorimer. By that time he had learned to appreciate craftsmanship in all its various forms - from the applied arts of Gothic Europe to nineteenth-century painting. Like Coats and Kay, Burrell also bought Old Master pictures and prints, including Dürer and Cranach the Elder, as well as Dutch, German and Italian decorative art, such as furniture, silver, glass and carpets. After 1900 the collector added Chinese ceramics to his shopping list.

From the beginning, Burrell was impressed by the skilful use of colour by artists such as Monticelli and the members of the Hague School. Alexander Reid encouraged him to purchase a certain amount of work by living artists, from French Impressionists to the local Glasgow Boys. Like Coats Burrell admired Joseph Crawhall's craftsmanship. During the 1890s his taste in fine art ran from Whistler (lithographs from Craibe Angus) to Jongkind (the painting *Fabrique de Cuirs Forts*, bought from Van Wisselingh). Both dealers also sold him works by the Maris brothers, including the lyrical *Butterflies* by Matthijs Maris (fig. 1.4), by whom Burrell owned no fewer than seventeen paintings. About Maris, Burrell

1.5 John W. Simpson and E.J. Milner Allen, Glasgow Art Gallery and Museum, designed 1892 and constructed 1894-1901. This photograph (Glasgow Museums and Art Galleries) was taken during the 1901 Glasgow International Exhibition.

wrote the following to the director of Glasgow Art Gallery, Tom Honeyman:

He is not everybody's painter but, nevertheless, he was a great genius. He was a dreamer and his pictures are poems in paint, full of feeling and tenderness and it was because I liked his work so much I bought it.[9]

In the mid-1890s Burrell bought both old and modern art from Alexander Reid. Besides pictures by Hogarth and Raeburn, Reid sold him Manet's *Portrait of Victorine Meurent* (Boston Museum of Fine Art) and several Whistlers, including *La Princesse du Pays de Porcelaine* (Freer Gallery, Washington), *The Fur Jacket* (Worcester Art Museum, Mass.), a *Nocturne* and a *Paysage*. But Burrell had little time for the *plein air* landscapes of the Impressionists, perhaps because he found their non-figural Realism empty. Nonetheless, he did support the contemporary artists of Glasgow, themselves influenced by French Naturalism. Then as now, mixing socially with artists had a certain cachet: when Burrell attended the party Reid gave to launch his new gallery in 1894, he was said to be proud of being the only non-artist present.[10]

By 1900, then, the average Glaswegian collector had developed a taste for recent, if not particularly avant-garde, French art. This was partly because of the new opportunities dealers offered them and partly the effect of recent work by Scottish artists, from the Glasgow Boys to the Edinburgh 'Impressionist' William McTaggart. In the early twentieth century William McInnes (1868-1944), partner in the shipping firm of Gow, Harrison &

Co., and Sir John Richmond (1869-1963), senior deputy chairman of his step-father's engineering firm G. & J. Weir, bought a great deal of French art from Reid (see cat. 2). Sir John's gift to Glasgow Art Gallery in 1949 included paintings by Antoine Vollon and Charles Conder as well as Samuel John Peploe, David Gauld and William Kennedy. His niece Isabel Traill presented part of her uncle's collection to the National Gallery of Scotland in 1979, including pictures by Boudin, Monet and Vuillard.

Sir John was an avid collector and, especially in later life, a prominent member of Glasgow society. He served as both chairman of the School of Art and president of the Royal Glasgow Institute of Fine Art. From the turn of the century the role of such institutions in the artistic life of the city was no less important than that of the galleries. As an institution, the Glasgow School of Art, housed for the whole of Richmond's collecting life in the famous building designed by Charles Rennie Mackintosh, dated back to the 1840s. As one of the government's Schools of Design, it had trained designers for industry, and helped manufacturers raise standards beyond mere mechanical expertise. Initially located in Ingram Street, the School subsequently occupied a corner of the Sauchiehall Street complex, which also housed the McLellan Galleries. A competition for the new School of Art, to be erected on a site in Renfrew Street, was held in early 1896. The first phase opened in 1899.

Similar plans for the expansion of the Corporation Galleries must have helped attract gifts and bequests. In 1888 the Glasgow International Exhibition had been held primarily to raise funds for a new Corporation museum and art gallery: in 1891 there was a competition for the design of a building to house the collections. At that stage there were also plans to incorporate a concert hall and the School of Art in the new building. However the organiser of the competition - the Association for the Promotion of Art and Music - ran out of funds. In 1894 construction began on the Kelvingrove galleries, today the principal museum and art gallery of Glasgow, according to a neo-baroque design by John W. Simpson and E.J. Milner Allen; the galleries opened in May 1901, as part of that year's Glasgow International Exhibition (fig. 1.5).

In the early 1900s Glasgow, like every other major British city, not only had a municipal art gallery and an art school but also several other institutions ruled by the established artists of the day. The importance of the Glasgow Institute of the Fine Arts within the cultural context of Glasgow is discussed by Roger Billcliffe in the next essay. From its inception in 1861 the Institute did much to promote contemporary painting, and the loan exhibitions it organised served to heighten appreciation of the Hague and Barbizon Schools. Like Reid's activities as an art dealer, the Institute contributed to the Europeanisation of Scottish art. Membership was available on subscription and the complaints of younger artists notwithstanding, it was a vital forum for artistic debate. A second society, the Glasgow Art Club, was founded in 1867 by a group of artists who sketched together, but by 1878, when it acquired permanent quarters, the Club had become a private institution for professionals. Restricted to elected male members, it was joined in 1882 by the Glasgow Society of Lady Artists, later the Lady Artists' Club. These societies gave painting a degree of social respectability, but they also tended to inhibit younger artists. It was not surprising, therefore, that in the 1880s and 1890s younger artists and designers formed groups to which contemporaries assigned such names as the 'Glasgow Boys' and 'The Four'. Their common purpose was to forge a new identity for Glasgow art and design. In their rejection of the status quo this generation of artists and designers, born in the third quarter of the nineteenth century, often looked far beyond Scotland for inspiration. Aspects of their contribution to European and more particularly Scottish culture are incorporated in the present exhibition.

Notes

1. Quoted by Elizabeth Williamson, Anne Riches and Malcolm Higgs, *The Buildings of Scotland: Glasgow,* London 1990, p. 159.

2. Frances Fowle, 'The Hague School and the Scots: a Taste for Dutch Pictures', *Apollo* (August 1991), pp. 108-111.

3. Richard Marks, *Burrell. Portrait of a Collector,* Glasgow (Richard Drew Publishing), 1983.

4. For a detailed discussion of the career of Alexander Reid, see Ronald Pickvance, *A Man of Influence: Alex Reid 1854-1928,* Edinburgh (Scottish Arts Council), 1968, pp. 5-16, and Vivien Hamilton, *Joseph Crawhall 1861-1913: One of the Glasgow Boys,* London (John Murray), 1990, pp. 94-97.

5. Vivien Hamilton, *op. cit.* (note 4), p. 98.

6. *Ibid.,* p. 96.

7. Richard Marks, *op. cit.* (note 3), p. 59.

8. Ronald Pickvance, *op. cit.* (note 4), p. 9.

9. Richard Marks, *op. cit.* (note 3), p. 75.

10. *Ibid.,* p. 72.

The Glasgow School of Painters

Roger Billcliffe

By the time Charles Rennie Mackintosh and his friends started exhibiting their work in Austria and Germany around 1900, Glasgow had already carved out a place for itself within the European art world. After 1914, however, the very aesthetics for which the city was noted fell out of fashion. By the 1950s, Glasgow was only remembered for not having supported its most gifted son. Another decade passed before Mackintosh was seen within the context of his native city's lively artistic milieu, and before the realisation dawned that a whole group of Scottish painters had preceded him - painters who were known not only in Europe but also in Canada and the United States.

In the 1850s, Glasgow was still living in the shadow of its smaller rival to the east. The presence of both the court and the government of Scotland had traditionally attracted artists to Edinburgh, but by the middle of the nineteenth century Glasgow, not Edinburgh, was the most vital city in Scotland.

The industrial revolution dealt Glasgow a mixed hand of cards. With its rich coal and iron deposits and its riverside location, the city soon became a major industrial centre on a global, as opposed to a Scottish or British, scale. Great wealth and awful poverty existed cheek by jowl, yet Glasgow helped the poor by improving the water supply and replacing the shanty towns that had sprung up to house the workers who streamed into the city from the Highlands and Ireland. Nonetheless, in social and cultural terms it still played second fiddle to Edinburgh; as regards the visual arts, the capital tightened its stranglehold to ward off any challenge from the upstart to the west.

There is more than a grain of truth in the assertion that Glasgow was culturally unsophisticated and unimaginative in the nineteenth century, and that it pandered to the lowest common denominator. The taste of the local collectors of modern art differed little from that of their counterparts in any English industrial city: they favoured amusing anecdote, history or genre painting of the most dispiriting kind. Glasgow's artists successfully satisfied this demand and had no financial motivation to exhibit their work at Scotland's premier venue, the Royal Scottish Academy. Of course there were artists with equally modest aspirations in Edinburgh as well, but the faculty of the Trustees' Academy was enough to attract the best young artists, who found they could support themselves handsomely by serving the needs of Edinburgh society. By now the path from the Royal Scottish Academy to London was well trod, and many of Scotland's painters chose artistic exile in the south. Like almost every self-made community, however, middle-class Glaswegians placed great emphasis on self-improvement. The same clever, hard-working men who had made their fortunes during the city's industrial and commercial renaissance turned their attention to the traditional pursuits of the rich. Their business often took them to London, where they witnessed the latest developments in contemporary painting and started buying. Seeing the taste of some of their clients change, dealers in Glasgow began to import pictures from the south. The more enlightened of these new collectors realised the best young artists were leaving to study in Edinburgh and London, since those cities offered not only greater opportunities but also a prestigious showcase for their work. In order to offset this trend, in 1861 a group of prominent artists and businessmen founded an institution that would hold exhibitions and encourage modern art in Glasgow.

The Glasgow Institute of the Fine Arts organised its first exhibition in 1861 in the McLellan Galleries, which were administered by Glasgow Corporation.[1] The exhibition was an immediate artistic and financial success. The organisers were astonished by the sheer quantity of work submitted. Though the artists who dominated the Glasgow Art Club also had a high profile in the Institute, the influential, open-minded laymen on the board of the Institute kept the door open to younger, less established, more provocative painters. The annual exhibition took its place on the artistic circuit alongside those organised by the Royal Academy, the Royal Scottish Academy, the West of England Academy, the Autumn Exhibition in Liverpool and so forth. The exhibitions grew in size as they did in quality.

The foundation of the Institute did little to mollify the Royal Scottish Academy's attitude toward painters from the west; indeed the two institutions became polarised in some respects, and each concentrated on work submitted by artists in its immediate environs. By the 1880s the Academy began enforcing an unofficial regulation that only artists who lived and worked in Edinburgh were eligible for membership, thus effectively barring artists from the rest of Scotland. On the other hand, the Institute had decided in the beginning that it was not exclusively interested in exhibiting local work. Their original intention was to bring the best of modern painting to Glasgow, whatever its origins, which they started doing by borrowing paintings from local collectors; John Graham lent them pictures by Turner and Constable, for instance. By the late 1870s the Institute was borrowing a great deal of French art that had recently entered Scottish collections. It recruited agents to seek out pictures in London, and by 1880 some of the most famous English artists were regularly exhibiting in Glasgow. Albert Moore, Millais, Holman Hunt, Poynter, Leighton, Watts and Burne-Jones joined Scots living in London such as Orchardson, MacWhirter and Farquharson in contributing major pictures to the exhibitions held annually at the Institute. French and Dutch paintings were either lent by collectors like James Donald and Sir Peter Coats, or contributed for

2.1 *James Guthrie,* A Funeral Service in the Highlands, *1881-82 (Glasgow Museums and Art Galleries)*

sale by the artists' dealers in London and Glasgow. Many works by Millet, Corot, Israels and Maris found a permanent home in Glasgow after appearing on the walls of the Institute.[1]

By 1879 the Institute had become so successful that it was able to commission premises of its own from one of Glasgow's leading architects, J.J. Burnet. The new building was one of the most attractive exhibition spaces in Britain and gave the Institute new status within the Scottish art world. Besides an annual exhibition it could now organise smaller shows at other times of the year as well; these often had a theme or were limited to particular media, such as watercolour, black and white or pastel. Membership in the Institute was not restricted to artists; life membership entailing certain privileges attracted collectors, and put the Institute on the social map of the city. The president was chosen from among the most prominent citizens of Glasgow and the west of Scotland generally; during approximately the first thirty years of the Institute's existence, the office was held by several of the city's leading industrialists, besides one of Britain's leading patrons, the Marquess of Bute. The more open policy espoused by the Institute gave younger artists, often excluded from membership in the Art Club and rejected by the Scottish Academy, the opportunity to display unconventional work. Even if the exhibitions were not exactly revolutionary, they did encourage catholic taste in a way many similar bodies under exclusively artistic control did not.

Against this background of artistic politics in Scotland a group of young men emerged in the mid-1880s who ultimately challenged the status quo in both major cities. They were dubbed the Glasgow School of Painters, a journalistic sobriquet that, like 'Impressionist', told only half the story. In Scotland, however, the term came to be synonymous with progressive painting. The artists themselves, not all of whom came from Glasgow or even worked there, could not agree on what to call themselves and finally settled on the more colloquial 'Boys'.[2] 'The Glasgow Boys', as they were popularly known, were never a homogeneous group who embraced a common artistic doctrine. Though they regularly participated in the same exhibitions, it was not until 1885 that a

collective vision or manner began to distinguish their work. Five years later they were invited to exhibit at the Grosvenor Gallery in London, but by that time they had already started down separate paths. By 1895 they had exhibited all over Europe and North America and, with few exceptions, no longer lived in Glasgow. By that time, however, their names were invariably identified with the city of Glasgow. As a result, the European art world was not surprised in 1900 when workaday Glasgow produced the likes of Charles Rennie Mackintosh.

If there is one central figure in the development of avant-garde painting in Glasgow in the 1880s, it is James Guthrie. Born the son of a minister in 1859, Guthrie resisted his family's pressure to study law. He was eventually apprenticed to the Scot John Pettie, well known in London for his elaborate historical or costume paintings.[3] Pettie's training at the Trustees' Academy accounts for the sophistication of his work, and helped compensate for the rather trite subjects he preferred. He was a master of the large, complicated figure compositions so fashionable at the time. Any apprentice in his studio would have received a thorough grounding in composition and in the traditional handling of paint which were taught by Scott Lauder at the Trustees' Academy. Guthrie spent almost two years in Pettie's London studio between 1879 and 1881, assisting the master, no doubt, but also working in the master's style. Each summer he returned to Scotland and, using Glasgow as his base, ventured into the

2.2 *Map of Scotland, showing locations where the Glasgow Boys worked. By permission of John Murray, publishers*

2.3 *John Lavery*, The Bridge at Grez (*private collection, photograph courtesy of The Fine Art Society, London*)

countryside to fill his sketchbook with the drawings and notes he used in the studio during the winter.

Guthrie's friend Edward Arthur Walton often accompanied him on these holiday sketching tours. The two artists had become acquainted in Glasgow before Guthrie left for London, and shared the distinction of having been refused membership by the Glasgow Art Club in the late 1870s. Walton studied in Düsseldorf and at the Glasgow School of Art; his work is distinguished by a continental emphasis on light and shade. Joseph Crawhall, the son of a talented sketcher and caricaturist who was related to Walton by marriage, occasionally joined Guthrie and Walton. Through his father's connections Crawhall had been able to work alongside the Punch illustrator Charles Keene. He visited the Pettie/Guthrie studio in London frequently, became a close friend of Guthrie's and occasionally even collaborated on canvases with him.

Despite Pettie's influence, Guthrie began to move away from the sort of anecdotal and costume pictures he had produced exclusively at the outset, and to work in a more realistic vein. Walton and Crawhall followed suit. Most of the paintings they produced in Scotland in the late 1870s and early 1880s are straightforward observations of specific landscapes, such as the beaches of the Clyde estuary, littered with upturned boats and fishing gear, the streets of Highland villages, with itinerant pedlars or children herding livestock, gypsy campfires smoking in the twilight, or farm labourers trudging to and from their work. These were all painted in a neutral manner, low in tone and devoid of social comment. From sketches he made at Brig o'Turk in Perthshire in the autumn of 1881 Guthrie produced a large painting that immediately attracted attention. One particularly adventurous, self-assured composition - *A Funeral Service in the Highlands* (1881, Glasgow Museums and Art Galleries, fig. 2.1) - shows how much he learnt from Pettie, who was a master of such crowded scenes. The artist's tonal control belies his youth. He deals with a popular and often mawkish subject, namely death, in a simple, straightforward manner,

recording the event rather than dramatising it.

On the opposite side of the country two other Glasgow painters were turning out similar paintings, oblivious of Guthrie's efforts. William York Macgregor and James Paterson had known each other from when they were in school. Both had come from relatively comfortable family backgrounds; indeed Macgregor's father owned one of Glasgow's most famous shipyards, and amassed such a large fortune that, unlike the other Boys, Macgregor did not have to earn a living. Having studied at the Slade School in London, at first Macgregor considered himself a cut above his peers in Glasgow. Like that of Paterson, who was trained in Paris, his early work is low in tone and concentrates on such typically realist subjects as street scenes, urban and rural landscapes, and even, in one case, a joiner's workshop, unlike the genre and costume pieces that were such a regular feature of the Institute's annual exhibitions. Like Guthrie and Walton, Macgregor and Paterson painted together in the summer and spent the winter in Glasgow (fig. 2.2). They worked up their sketches or small canvases into larger paintings suitable for the big exhibitions, where it was difficult for small formats to compete alongside the *grandes machines* of the more established artists. Thanks to his financial independence, Macgregor could afford the luxury of a spacious studio in Glasgow, where he hosted all the Boys. Since Guthrie did not often visit the studio, Macgregor naturally assumed the role of mentor to the younger men. It was probably during the evenings in Macgregor's studio that Paterson's stories about Parisian ateliers inspired another group of young men (the third small clique at the Institute's annual exhibition in 1885) to follow his footsteps to the French capital.[4]

John Lavery, Thomas Millie Dow, Alexander Roche and William Kennedy all spent time in Paris between 1882 and 1885. More importantly, they all lived part of the summer in the Barbizon village of Grez-sur-Loing, an artists' colony that attracted not only French and British but also Irish, American and Scandinavian artists (figs. 2.3, 2.4, 2.5). In the 1870s

2.4 *John Lavery*, On the Loing, an Afternoon Chat, *1884 (photograph reproduced with kind permission of the Trustees of the Ulster Museum, Belfast)*

2.5 *William Kennedy,* Spring, *1884 (Paisley Museum and Art Galleries, Renfrew District Council)*

2.6 *Edward A. Walton,* A Berwickshire Fieldworker, *1884 (Tate Gallery, London)*

the critic R.A. Macaulay Stevenson and his cousin Robert Louis Stevenson had stayed at Grez, and it now became a favourite retreat of the English naturalist painter, William Stott of Oldham.[5] Stott and the young French painter Jules Bastien-Lepage (fig. 2.13 and cat.1) must be responsible for the radical change in style and subject matter of these four young Scots. Genre and subject pictures had been their mainstay. Lavery's goal as an artist was doubtless financial and social success; his early work is unashamedly sentimental and melodramatic, unlike that of the artists centred on Guthrie and Macgregor. Given the fact that Lavery, who had no other source of income, painted for the market, it seems surprising that after two summers in Grez his art became more radical than that of almost all the other Boys.

Guthrie and Walton, and probably Macgregor and Paterson, also encountered the work of Bastien-Lepage by 1882 at the latest. The Frenchman's influence can most easily be detected in the work of all of the Boys after that date (figs. 2.6, 2.7), but it certainly does not account for their original interest in Realism. Most of the Boys had been painting Realist subjects from the late 1870s, almost certainly inspired by the paintings of Holl, Herkomer and the two Scots, John and Thomas Faed. The Faeds' sentimentality notwithstanding, their contemporary subjects offered young Scottish painters an alternative to the gimcrackery of many of the artists around them. The detail, the self-assured use of tone and colour, and the sheer craftsmanship of their work was an ideal model for Guthrie, Macgregor and other

members of the group. It was, however, an essentially academic kind of painting still attuned to the annual exhibition circuit. Though, like the Faeds, they often exploited a particular situation for heightened moral or sentimental effect, the Boys never expressed any political views. In their frequent depictions of the rural poor they preferred honesty to mawkishness. The Boys did not practise Courbet's brand of radical Realism, even though some of them had absorbed the example of James McNeill Whistler, a painter who had known Courbet and offered another dimension to the growing interest in contemporary subjects. Whistler influenced the Boys in many different ways. Especially in the face of hostility and derision, they drew inspiration from his masterly use of tone in his 'harmonies' and 'symphonies', from the strong sense of design about his compositions and, above all, from his conviction that the artist had the right to choose his own subject matter and, before all others, to please himself.

To have responded so readily to the Naturalist paintings of Bastien-Lepage, the Boys must have been aware of Realists such as the Barbizon painters. Pictures by Millet and Diaz could be seen in the Institute's exhibitions in 1880, and in 1882 Guthrie and Walton almost certainly saw the paintings from the Paris Salon exhibited at The Fine Art Society in London. The latter exhibition included *The Ferry* by Stott of Oldham (fig. 2.8), painted at Grez, which must have convinced them of Bastien-Lepage's impact; indeed the Frenchman's work was on display at several London locations during the summer of 1882.[6] Guthrie and his friends were working that summer in the Lincolnshire village, from which London would have been much more easily accessible than from their usual summer haunts in the remote countryside of Scotland. Much of their work from this period reflects a growing interest in rural landscape and daily life. Guthrie and Crawhall both returned to their winter studios with the germ of a major painting in their sketchbooks. Crawhall's *A Lincolnshire Pasture* (fig. 2.9) is one of the first of his 'animal portraits'. A rare oil painting - he worked predominantly in pastels and watercolours - its strong horizontals echo the composition of Stott's *Ferry,* down to the stripes of grass in the foreground, water in the middle distance and blue sky above the stark horizon. Guthrie also had in mind a composition divided into dominant horizontal bands, but the final product owed as much to Bastien-Lepage as to Stott. Despite its antecedents, *To Pastures New* (fig. 2.10) is not simply a slavish imitation of French painting. Its bright sunlight, strong shadows and clear sense of movement across the canvas are alien to both Stott and Bastien-Lepage. The work shows Guthrie's clear understanding of Naturalist technique and his ability to adapt them to Scottish tradition. Though it was not exhibited in Glasgow until 1885, *To Pastures New* ensured

2.7 *Edward A. Walton,* The Herd Boy, *1886 (collection Andrew McIntosh Patrick, photograph courtesy of The Fine Art Society, London)*

2.8 *William Stott,* The Ferry, *c. 1882 (private collection, photograph courtesy of The Fine Art Society, London)*

2.9 *Joseph Crawhall,* A Lincolnshire Pasture, *1882 (City of Dundee Museums and Art Galleries Department)*

2.10 *James Guthrie,* To Pastures New, *1883 (City of Aberdeen Art Gallery and Museums Collections)*

Guthrie's supremacy within the group.

Macgregor had spent the winter of 1882-83 finishing a large painting of a costermonger counting her earnings beside her stall.[7] It was an unusual subject for the Boys, being an urban rather than a rural scene. Macgregor left it in his studio and went to spend the summer in Crail, where he painted a series of fine Naturalist paintings of that Fife village, showing its inhabitants basking in clear sunlight, which are reminiscent of Guthrie's *To Pastures New*. After returning to Glasgow he painted out the figure of the coster and replaced her with more vegetables. The large format of *The Vegetable Stall* (fig. 2.11) is enigmatic, given its unassuming subject.[8] Macgregor had almost certainly seen *To Pastures New* at the Royal Academy in London in 1883, and realised his own efforts at figure painting did not measure up. He must have painted out the figure in the winter of 1883-84 (the finished picture is dated 1884) to avoid unfavourable comparisons. The artist kept the painting hidden in his studio, and though it remains one of the key works of the Glasgow School, the canvas was not exhibited publicly until after the artist's death, when his widow presented it to the National Gallery of Scotland.

The Vegetable Stall is not as patently indebted to Bastien-Lepage as *To Pastures New*. Guthrie's adoption of the square brush, a Bastien-Lepage trademark, distinguished him as a disciple of the young French academic painter, as did his denial of any linear perspective in his paintings and his insistence on a form of 'aerial' perspective achieved through skilful brushwork. Other indications that his work was inspired by Bastien-Lepage include the highly finished hands and faces, the horizontal elements - particularly to emphasise the horizon, which is often situated high in the composition - and,

2.11 *William Y. Macgregor,* The Vegetable Stall, *1884 (National Gallery of Scotland, Edinburgh)*

2.12 *James Guthrie,* The Hind's Daughter, *1883 (National Gallery of Scotland, Edinburgh)*

above all, the position of the central figure on the picture plane. Despite the confidence of Bastien-Lepage's peers and teachers that he would become a successful member of the French artistic establishment, his failure to win the Prix de Rome prompted him to reassess his career. Retreating to his native village of Damvillers, east of Rheims, he assumed the role of village painter, recording the daily lives of his family and friends, the labourers in the fields and the beggars in the streets. Wanting to emulate Bastien-Lepage, Guthrie settled in the Berwickshire village of Cockburnspath in 1883. James Paterson had already moved to Moniaive in Dumfriesshire, where he painted his neighbours and the surrounding countryside. Walton and Crawhall joined Guthrie at Cockburnspath, as did another young Glaswegian, George Henry, and the slightly older, more experienced Edinburgh painter, Arthur Melville, who had also studied in Paris and Grez. At the end of the summer all of them returned to the city, except for Guthrie, who stayed on in Cockburnspath, determined to immerse himself in country life. He went on sketching in the fields, planning large and complicated compositions on small panels and in his sketchbook, many of which came to naught. Disappointed by his failure to regain his former confidence - evident in such works as *A Funeral Service in the Highlands* - he finally left the village in 1885. Yet his compositions of single figures and small groups are superb. *The Hind's Daughter* (fig. 2.12) and *Schoolmates* (1884-85, Musée des Beaux-Arts, Ghent) evince Guthrie's grasp of Bastien-Lepage's Naturalism (fig. 2.13 and cat. 1). The technique and composition of these canvases are

unrivalled by such British Naturalists as George Clausen, Henry Herbert la Thangue and the group of painters associated with the village of Newlyn in Cornwall. Working in isolation, away from his friends in Glasgow, it was Guthrie who produced the period's masterpieces.

In France, meanwhile, Lavery, Kennedy and Roche were working towards similar ends. Lavery had given up his trite genre paintings, though in the last of these, Bastien-Lepage's influence was apparent in his use of a square brush and Naturalist manner. In Grez all three artists adopted the same attitude to village life as Guthrie had in Cockburnspath, and produced a fine series of paintings composed and handled in the style of French Naturalism. Many of these paintings were shown at the Glasgow Institute in 1885, alongside Guthrie's *To Pastures New,* when critics and collectors realised there was something afoot in Scotland. Guthrie returned from Cockburnspath that year, as did Lavery from Grez. The latter's *Bridge at Grez* (1883, Private Collection) and *On the Loing - an Afternoon Chat* (1884, Ulster Museum, Belfast) vied with *To Pastures New* for supremacy, but in the end both artists lost, as their work did not sell at the exhibition. Despite critical acclaim and a few brickbats, few collectors wished to hang such paintings on their walls. Though the Boys made no overt social commentary, the Scottish bourgeoisie did not consider their subject matter suitable for their drawing rooms. This came as a grave blow to the artists, who saw themselves not as political or social commentators, but simply as followers of an artistic style that could be traced to one man's reaction to life in rural France. With the exception of Macgregor, all of them depended upon the sale of their work; yet there was no denying the fact that their principal clients, the growing band of collectors in Glasgow, were not impressed.

The first to find a way out of this dilemma was Lavery. Given his ambition and personal finances, he took a pragmatic attitude toward painting. Reasoning that subject matter, not style, was hurting sales, he turned his attention from the rural underprivileged to the bourgeoisie. His Naturalist paintings of middle-class subjects were successful from the start. Indeed one of his first endeavours is another masterpiece of the Glasgow School: *A Tennis Party* (fig. 2.14), one of the most remarkable British pictures of the 1880s. The sense of movement apparent in Lavery's more spontaneous sketches, such as *A Rally* (cat. 34), together with the originality of his subjects and the freshness of his Naturalist technique, all assured him of success. Every one of the tennis players could easily be recognised. The reaction of both press and public was favourable. Lavery was taken up by Glasgow society, whose younger members in particular were fond of his informal style of portraiture.

Building on the success of his new-found formula,

2.13 Jules Bastien-Lepage, Pauvre Fauvette, *1881 (Glasgow Museums and Art Galleries) cat. 1*

Lavery responded to the Glasgow International Exhibition in 1888 by recording it in a series of paintings (fig. 2.15 and cat. 35). All rather low key, the fifty or so canvases were displayed at the end of the Exhibition and sold immediately. Fireworks, musical rides by the cavalry, gondolas on the river, ladies taking tea, cigar vendors and flower girls were all part of the artist's widening repertoire.

In the middle of the Exhibition Lavery was commissioned to paint a large composition of Queen Victoria's visit, making 1888 truly an *annus mirabilis* for him. He planned the canvas with the help of his camera - which he had learned to use as a Glasgow photographer's assistant - and his sketchbook, but it was over two years before the finished painting could be unveiled. Comprising recognisable portraits of over a hundred dignitaries and guests, it established Lavery's reputation in Scotland as a portrait painter. Even this triumph could not slake the artist's ambition, however; before long he moved to London, where he became a neighbour and friend of Whistler, and won acclaim as a society portraitist.

Guthrie did not adopt Lavery's new subject matter, even though he had begun to have serious problems with his work during the last months he spent in Cockburnspath. Difficulties with a large canvas of field-workers sheltering during a storm threw him into a severe depression, during which he seriously considered putting down his brush forever and returning to the life of an academic. His cousins' timely commission to paint a portrait of their father distracted the disgruntled artist from his problems and for the next few years he concentrated on portraiture and pastels, often selecting the same middle-class subjects with which Lavery had had so much success. Yet his painting of *Old Willie - a Village Worthy* (fig. 2.16 and cat. 21) and his pastels of hay - making and ploughing contrast notably with the musical evenings and tennis games he also exhibited in 1890. His efforts found little favour in London, but in Glasgow, where they were subsequently shown, all fifty or so of them were sold.

Old Willie had been painted in the town of Kirkcudbright, in the region of southwest Scotland known as Galloway. It was there that Guthrie's spirits had been lifted when he visited two other young artists who had become naturalist painters. One of these, George Henry, had worked alongside Guthrie for some years and spent at least one summer with him in Berwickshire, painting in such fishing villages as Eyemouth. The other, Edward Atkinson Hornel, had studied in Antwerp, but adopted the square brush and Naturalist manner on returning to Scotland in 1885. Hornel was devoted to his adoptive Kirkcudbright and it was probably there that he met Guthrie and Henry in 1885. Henry and Hornel became firm friends and regular correspondents; in the pictures they exchanged they recognised a mutual feeling for design, pattern and colour. It was precisely

2.14 John Lavery, The Tennis Party,
*1885 (City of Aberdeen Art Gallery
and Museum Collections)*

2.15 *John Lavery,* The Glasgow International Exhibition, *1888 (Glasgow Museums and Art Galleries) cat. 35*

these three elements in the work of one of the Glasgow School's most original painters - Arthur Melville - that inspired them.

Melville may have also inspired Guthrie's series of pastels, but the members of the group on whom he had the most direct influence were Hornel and Henry. He had visited Guthrie at Cockburnspath several times. Though he lived, and had been trained, in Edinburgh, he found the closed minds of the capital's artistic establishment too stifling for his natural rebelliousness. He had first visited France in 1879 and was regularly in Grez in the early 1880s. Lavery and his friends may have learned of Grez from pictures Melville had exhibited at the Glasgow Institute. In 1882 he left France and journeyed to Karachi by way of North Africa and the Middle East. In his sketchbook he recorded the sights and experiences of the next eighteen months, making quick studies in fluid, glowing watercolours. On his return he worked these up into large pictures, occasionally in oil but usually in watercolour. The intense colour of Melville's watercolours, his technique - dubbed 'blottesque' - and the drama and novelty of his subject matter, attracted immediate attention. Having produced Realist paintings in Scotland and France for some time, he sympathised somewhat with what the Boys were doing, but most of his work in oil and watercolour is so alien to the tenets of Naturalism that one wonders what drew these artists so close together. If they were not bound by style, then they must have been by their opposition to the artistic hierarchy of Scotland. Since Melville was slightly older and infinitely more experienced in the ways of the world, the Boys admired him, and were encouraged by his visits to Cockburnspath. The effect of these visits on Henry and Hornel, however, was more substantial.

Melville's clear, bright colours and his method of heightening the paper's tone with Chinese white lent his work a certain intensity (fig. 2.17 and cat. 49). The impact of his subject matter was further enhanced by his almost symbolic use of colour. Though they both produced work in a classic Naturalist manner, Hornel and Henry were primarily colourists who found new solutions in Melville's work. In Kirkcudbright and the surrounding woods they began making a series of paintings in which the texture of the paint, the patterns in the composition and the symbolic colours became, in and of themselves, more important than the ostensible subject of the picture. Horizons, generally high in Naturalist paintings, disappeared altogether; there is something oppressive about the arrangement of figures, trees and landscapes in these paintings, which were executed between 1887 and 1889. These works resemble nothing else painted in Britain at the time; indeed the only conceivable parallels are with Gauguin and the Pont Aven painters. We cannot know whether the two Scots were familiar with the

work of those artists, but they may have visited Paris with Guthrie, Walton and Melville in 1889, when Guthrie won a medal at the Paris Salon. These small studies culminated in three large paintings, however, one of which was made by Henry and two by the artists jointly between 1888 and 1891. Though *A Galloway Landscape* (fig. 2.18 and cat. 27) is one of the Boys' masterpieces by any account, it is still highly enigmatic. The stream snaking sinuously across the hillside and the inconsistencies in scale between stream, cattle and trees recall Pont Aven painting of the period. The disposition of the various elements and the two-dimensional pattern they form is reminiscent of Gauguin and his circle. Yet the effect of sunlight, created by the intense colour of the sky, owes more to the Glasgow Naturalist painting of the mid-1880s. The dichotomy between the archetypal imagery of a Galloway hillside and the more straightforward imagery of the Glasgow School's rustic Naturalism - between Symbolism and Realism, in other words - creates tension. This tension is maintained throughout the composition by an intuitive use of colour and pattern that is more suggestive than descriptive.

The two joint pictures - *The Druids: Bringing in the Mistletoe* (fig. 2.19 and cat. 29) and *The Star in the East* (1891, Glasgow Museums and Art Galleries) - show how closely Hornel and Henry collaborated. In their preoccupation with pattern, historical iconography, colour and texture they moved away from Glasgow School painting of the mid-1880s. Most of the other Boys had also done so, but none so radically. Hornel was almost certainly responsible for choosing their new subject matter; as an avid local historian he was fascinated with the Druidic culture

2.16 *James Guthrie,* Old Willie - a Village Worthy, *1886 (Glasgow Museums and Art Galleries) cat. 21*

2.17 Arthur Melville,
A Mediterranean Port, 1892
(Glasgow Museums and Art
Galleries) cat. 49

event the exhibition attracted a great deal of attention from the press, as the Grosvenor had played a prominent role in promoting avant-garde English painting in the 1880s. The exhibition included *The Druids: Bringing in the Mistletoe* (fig. 2.19 and cat. 29) as well as more Naturalist canvases painted by the Boys in the mid-1880s. The critics welcomed what they saw as the emergence of a new school whose manner was quite different from most contemporary English painting.[9] The exhibition was also witnessed by two painters from Munich, who had been sent to London to find new work for the annual exhibition of the Munich Art Society. Seventeen of the Boys were invited to show their work that year in the Bavarian capital; their submissions ranged in style from Lavery's *Bridge at Grez* to the more symbolic, joint works of Hornel and Henry.

In 1893 the Art Society suffered the first of the secessions that were to sweep the European artistic establishment in the 1890s. The Boys were invited to send work to the new Secession, thus strengthening their credentials as exponents of the avant-garde. This was followed by invitations from kindred organisations across Europe. Lavery's *Tennis Party* was acquired by the Pinakothek in Munich in 1890 (subsequently de-accessioned in a fit of pre-1914 anti-British sentiment) and other works were bought by museums in Leipzig, Weimar, Stuttgart and Budapest. Examples of Glasgow painting were displayed in Dresden, Cologne, Berlin, St Petersburg (in an exhibition organised by Diaghilev), Vienna, Venice, Brussels, Bruges and Barcelona. Charles Kurtz of the St Louis Exposition saw their work in Barcelona in 1894; he had hoped to bring it to St Louis later that year, but since it was too late he selected paintings that were to be shown in Chicago, Cincinnati and New York when he returned to Europe the following year. In the late 1890s the Boys went to the United States again, exhibiting their work in such cities as Pittsburgh, where Lavery's *Bridge at Grez* was purchased by a museum.

The Boys' success abroad had repercussions in

of Galloway. The artist's other passion was Japan, a passion he most probably acquired from Whistler; indeed, after 1890 both artists began making specific references to Japanese culture. *The Brook* (fig. 2.20) was one of Hornel's first pictures with figures wearing Japanese costumes. The line traced across the canvas by the brook calls to mind the stream in *The Galloway Landscape,* but the *genius loci* so palpable in Henry's picture is confused here by dressing the girls *à la japonaise* in order to underscore the effect of pattern. The picture had far-reaching influence since it was bought by J. Herbert MacNair - close friend, colleague and future brother-in-law of Charles Rennie Mackintosh. Subsequent pictures by Hornel further explore Japanese themes, culminating in *Summer* (fig. 2.21), which shows two Galloway cowherds, dressed in full Japanese costume, chasing a butterfly - that quintessentially Whistlerian symbol of the 1890s - as their livestock stray into forbidden pastures.

The colour, movement and explicit pattern of *Summer* bring the Glasgow School to a perfect close. Afterwards Hornel and Henry took the ultimate art tour, a visit to Japan. Leaving Glasgow in February 1893, they spent a total of eighteen months in the country, and returned with watercolours and oils that bore the first signs of stylistic disunity between the two men. Many of Henry's oils were damaged on the way home, but his surviving watercolours reveal a return to a more Naturalist manner, low in key and cool in harmony. Hornel, on the other hand, revelled in the colour and vivacity of Japanese life, as evidenced by the paintings he made there. The exhibition of their work in Glasgow in 1896 was one of the last times the Glasgow Boys were featured so prominently on their own turf.

Many of the Boys had hoped to rise to the top of their profession, not only in Scotland but also in Britain. In the 1890s they earned an international reputation shared by few of their British contemporaries. In the late 1880s the Boys had taken part in a variety of London exhibitions, most notably at the New English Art Club. In 1890, moreover, Sir Coutts Lindsay invited them to participate in an exhibition at his Grosvenor Gallery, intended to be the final exhibition before Lindsay closed it. In the

2.18 George Henry, A Galloway Landscape, 1889 (Glasgow Museums and Art Galleries) cat. 27

Scotland. As early as 1888 the Royal Scottish Academy had offered an olive branch to the Glasgow artists by dropping its residency requirements and awarding Guthrie Associate Membership. Walton and Lavery received recognition next. By the mid-1890s most of the Boys had been recognised by the RSA. Guthrie was subsequently elected Vice-president and President in a sincere attempt to heal the rift between the Glasgow and Edinburgh artistic fraternities.

Success brought new pressures to bear on the Boys, as Glasgow had neither the size nor the sophistication to support such a talented and prolific group of painters. Gradually the lure of London, and even Edinburgh, proved too much for the artists. Walton left for Chelsea in 1893, where he lived next door to his old hero Whistler. Guthrie and Lavery followed shortly. Though their links with Glasgow were never entirely broken, their individual futures lay elsewhere.

Glasgow had not responded quickly enough to what the Boys had to offer. They had their faithful band of supporters in the city, but Glasgow's collectors had never had quite enough courage to endorse the artists as their careers took shape. The next generation of local painters did not suffer the same fate. Though Mackintosh, the true genius of the period, failed to attract patrons, being an architect his situation was different. But the Boys had successfully

convinced the artistic community that artistic freedom was an inviolable right. They helped abolish the blinkered attitude toward studying, working and exhibiting abroad. Most importantly they impressed on Glasgow's artists the fact that their work could arouse interest beyond the confines of their home town, thus engendering a new self-confidence that sustained subsequent generations. Mackintosh benefited directly from this: hailing from a city whose artistic credentials had already been established abroad facilitated his progress. Indeed it was Mackintosh and his fellow designers and architects - not the city's artists - who assumed the mantle left behind by the Glasgow Boys.

Painting in Glasgow from the 1890s was undoubtedly much better than it had been in the 1870s. Artists like William Alfred Gibson and William Wells maintained the Boys' high standards. One of the younger artists associated with the Boys, David Young Cameron, began experimenting with etching in the late 1880s, and later played an important role in the technique's revival that distinguished British art of the early twentieth century. Cameron was obviously inspired by Whistler, but he was especially interested in Meryon and Piranesi, as was another young Glaswegian, Muirhead Bone. After studying architecture Bone turned to printmaking and specialised in architectural subjects such as views of the Clyde, London and

2.19 George Henry and Edward A. Hornel, The Druids: Bringing in the Mistletoe, *1890 (Glasgow Museums and Art Galleries) cat. 29*

2.20 Edward A. Hornel, The Brook, *1890 (Hunterian Art Gallery, University of Glasgow)*

2.21 *Edward A. Hornel,* Summer, *1891 (The Board of Trustees of the National Museums and Galleries on Merseyside, Walker Art Gallery, Liverpool)*

New York. A master of the burin, Bone produced intensely dramatic drypoints, powerful images of railway stations, bridges and busy construction sites around the new Manhattan skyscrapers. Cameron and Bone won international acclaim for their etchings and were among the select group of British artists commissioned to record the Great War. Along with other Scots, such as James McBey and William Douglas McLeod, they revitalised the art of printmaking, extending Glasgow's international reputation into yet another aspect of the visual arts. In the 1890s, however, much of the city's most talented youth was more attracted to the decorative

arts, design and architecture.

One man, John Quinton Pringle, bridged the gap between the painters and the designers. Often described as an amateur, in fact Pringle studied at Glasgow School of Art, where he attended evening classes, as Mackintosh and several of the Boys had done. Ultimately, however, he chose the security of an optician over the insecurity of an artist. He learned a great deal from the square brush technique of Glasgow Naturalism and drew his subject matter from the everyday reality of the city around him. His painting *Muslin Street, Bridgeton* (fig. 2.22 and cat. 56) shows the bustling streets of Glasgow from his

2.22 John Q. Pringle, Muslin Street, Bridgeton, 1895 (Edinburgh City Museums and Art Galleries) cat. 56

of one of the busiest, noisiest, smokiest cities, that with its like fellows make up the sum-total of the greatness of Britain's commercial position, there is a movement existing, and a compelling force behind it ... which ... may yet, perhaps, put Glasgow on the Clyde into the hand of the future historian of Art, on much the same grounds as those on which Bruges, Venice and Amsterdam find themselves in the book of the life of the world.[10]

workshop, a subject rarely tackled by the Boys but one that appealed increasingly to Pringle. The appearance and disappearance of the figures and the use of trees and architecture as framing devices recalls the tapestry-like quality of Hornel and Henry's Galloway paintings (see Pringle's *Two Figures and a Fence,* cat. 60). Following the Boys' example, Pringle visited France and painted in Normandy. His exposure to the work of artists such as Seurat and Signac, which we cannot prove, might account for the pointillist technique he ultimately adopted. Be that as it may, Pringle remains an enigma. Like Mackintosh, he was patronised by William Davidson, who collected Glasgow School painting; this may explain the decorative quality about his work.

In 1891 the Corporation of Glasgow acceded to pressure from the Boys to purchase Whistler's famous portrait of Thomas Carlyle. It was a rare civic acknowledgement of the artists' reputation among their fellow citizens. Sadly, Glasgow never took the opportunity to acquire many of their major works. It was perhaps in recognition of this omission that, in 1899, the Boys were asked to paint a series of murals in the banqueting hall of the magnificent City Chambers. Ten years earlier, in *The Scottish Art Review* - which owed its existence to the Boys - they had been recommended for the commission as the Chambers were being built. Had they received it at that time, they might have painted very different murals and been more committed to their home town. Whatever its subject, a Naturalist masterpiece in the City Chambers might have led to still other public commissions and inspired confidence in the newcomers. As it happened, the murals are not a worthy memorial to some of Glasgow's most illustrious artists. Their reputation was secure, however; the success they achieved for themselves and for Glasgow far exceeded their expectations in 1880. As Francis Newbery put it in the introduction to the book David Martin wrote about the Boys in 1897:

And at the end of the nineteenth century, in the midst

Notes

1. On the history of the Institute see *The Royal Glasgow Institute of the Fine Arts, 1861-1989* (compiled by Roger Billcliffe), Glasgow 1990.

2. Letter from R. Macaulay Stevenson to Dr T.J. Honeyman, 9 January 1941, quoted in J. Reid *et al., The Glasgow Art Club, 1867-1967,* Glasgow 1967.

3. For a full biography of Guthrie see James L. Caw, *Sir James Guthrie: a Biography,* London 1932.

4. Paterson received his formal training in the Parisian ateliers of Jean-Paul Laurens and Jacquesson de la Chevreuse, who must have taught him the importance of *les valeurs.* See James Paterson, 'The Art Student in Paris', *The Scottish Art Review* (October 1888), pp. 118-120.

5. See R.L. Stevenson, 'Fontainebleau: Village Communities of Painters, IV', *Magazine of Art* 2 (1884), p. 345.

6. For a discussion of the appearance of Bastien-Lepage's work in London in the early 1880s, see K. McConkey, 'The Bouguereau of the Naturalists - Bastien-Lepage and British Art', *Art History* 1.3 (1978), pp. 371-382.

7. *The Bailie,* Glasgow, 25 April 1883.

8. The figure is visible on X-rays of the painting taken by the Conservation Department of the National Galleries of Scotland.

9. Reviews appeared in *The Magazine of Art, The Saturday Review* and *The Spectator,* 10 May 1890.

10. David Martin, *The Glasgow School of Painting,* London 1897; with an introduction by Francis H. Newbery.

Biographical notes

Sir David Muirhead Bone
1876-1953

The son of a journalist, Muirhead Bone was born in Partick, Glasgow. He abandoned his training as an architect in favour of a more precarious career as a draughtsman. Within ten years of the first, self-taught etchings and drypoints he made in 1895, he had established himself as a distinguished printmaker. In 1897 Muirhead Bone was elected to the Glasgow Art Club and three years later moved to Ayr, where he taught art. His first London exhibition was held at the Carfax Gallery in 1902. His etchings of the 1901 Glasgow International Exhibition were published by T. & R. Annan and Sons, the Glasgow photographers and publishers. Thenceforth Muirhead Bone worked almost exclusively in drypoint.

Early in his career Bone most admired Dutch masters such as Van der Heyden and Ruysdael. Between 1910 and 1912, however, he made his first extensive visit to Italy. The artist's Italian prints are dramatic, but thanks to his careful use of chiaroscuro they have a sense of balance and order. These attributes, together with his fascination with building construction, were perhaps a legacy of his early training. Muirhead Bone also visited other parts of Europe, including the Netherlands in 1913, and during both World Wars he served as an official artist. His prodigious oeuvre totalled more than five hundred etchings, drypoints and lithographs, and many thousands of drawings and watercolours.

Like D.Y. Cameron, Muirhead Bone also had a distinguished public career. He was appointed a trustee of both the National Gallery and the Tate Gallery, and knighted in 1937. Sir David held honorary degrees from the universities of St Andrews, Glasgow, Liverpool and Oxford.

Sir David Young Cameron
1865-1945

The son of a Glasgow minister, D.Y. Cameron embarked on a commercial career on leaving school, while attending the Glasgow School of Art in the evenings. At the age of twenty he enrolled in the Trustees' Academy in Edinburgh. His painting style in the 1890s was heavily influenced by Velasquez, Whistler, the Barbizon painters and Matthijs Maris. Though a skilled painter in oils and watercolours, he is principally remembered as one of Britain's foremost etchers. George Stevenson, an etcher friend of Seymour Haden, encouraged him to take up the medium in 1889. His early etchings, including the Paisley Set (1888), the Clyde Set (1889) and especially his North Italian Set (1896), were predominantly Whistlerian. By 1905 he was making drypoint additions to his etchings to achieve greater depth. As far as his prints are concerned, after 1911 he worked exclusively in drypoint.

The artistic qualities of Cameron's prints carried over into his paintings, which capture the grandeur of the Scottish landscape in striking contrasts of light and shade. An active supporter of all the visual arts, Cameron's collection of contemporary British art covered various media, such as sculpture by Alfred Gilbert. Deeply religious, he promoted the craft of ecclesiastical stained glass, which indeed became his lasting legacy to Scottish design.

Cameron was a member of the Glasgow Arts Club from 1891. He was elected ARSA in 1904, RSW in 1915, ARA in 1916, RSA in 1918 and RA in 1920. Knighted in 1924, he received numerous honorary doctorates from British universities. In 1933 he was appointed the King's Painter and Limner in Scotland; the position had previously been held by Sir Henry Raeburn and Sir David Wilkie, and was an acknowledgement of his notable contribution to Scottish art.

Joseph Crawhall
1861-1913

Thomas Millie Dow
1848-1919

David Gauld
1865-1936

Joseph Crawhall was born in Morpeth, Northumberland. His father, a rope manufacturer and artist-writer, taught him to draw from memory. After finishing his schooling in England he worked in Morot's Paris atelier, but left after only two months. He became acquainted with James Guthrie and E.A. Walton (whose brother Richard married Crawhall's sister) in 1879. His earliest oils, including pastoral scenes painted with Guthrie in Lincolnshire in 1881, already display flair, fresh colours and open brushwork. Crawhall experimented with various media: he preferred gouache but tried his hand occasionally at watercolour, adding a bit of bodycolour to it. He applied paint thinly, and used 'brown holland' canvas in order to achieve the maximum pictorial effect.

From 1884 until 1893 Crawhall spent much of his time in Tangier. His North African watercolours are fluent, their colours rich. With their shorthand notation of form and the immediate appeal of their subject, his many bird and animal studies attracted the attention of dealers and collectors in Glasgow in the 1890s. Though he was on the periphery of the Glasgow School, Crawhall probably had less difficulty selling his work in the city than his associates. Alex Reid was both a friend and dealer, William Burrell one of his principal patrons. Crawhall died in London.

Thomas Millie Dow, son of the town clerk of Dysart in Fife, studied painting in Edinburgh, and in Paris with Gérôme at the Académie des Beaux-Arts and Carolus Duran at the Académie Julian. From 1880 he exhibited landscapes and flowerpieces at the GIFA, turning in 1893 to more romantic, allegorical figural subjects. A friend of William Stott of Oldham, he was primarily a decorative artist who used colour with the utmost sensitivity, and without the bravura of many Glasgow painters. In 1897, the year he settled in Glasgow, he joined the NEAC. Millie Dow travelled extensively, wintering in Italy, Tangier and Canada. He was among the first of the Glasgow painters to leave Scotland, settling in St Ives in Cornwall in 1895.

David Gauld was born in Glasgow. He was apprenticed to the lithographers Gilmour & Dean while studying part-time at the School of Art until 1885 and again in 1889. In 1887 he joined the staff of the *Glasgow Weekly Citizen* to illustrate the novels that the newspaper serialised. At once economic and decorative, Gauld's style was influenced by the Pre-Raphaelite Dante Gabriel Rossetti and the Dutchman Jacob Maris. In 1896 the artist visited Grez, where he painted a series of atmospheric landscapes. Yet his approach to art was essentially that of a designer. Much of his best work of the 1890s was two-dimensional and richly coloured - ideally suited to stained glass. From the early 1890s he supplied the Glasgow firm of J. & W. Guthrie with designs. During that decade he shared a studio with Harrington Mann, who designed for the same firm. Gauld's most important glass commission (1900-1910) was for St Andrew's Church in Buenos Aires. Toward the end of his life, in 1935, he was appointed director of Design Studies at the Glasgow School of Art.

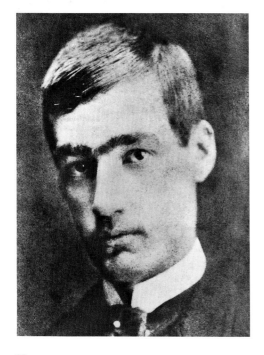

Sir James Guthrie
1859-1930

George F. Henry
1858-1943

Edward Atkinson Hornel
1864-1933

Born in Greenock, James Guthrie was the youngest son of an evangelical clergyman, Dr John Guthrie. Encouraged by the history painter James Drummond, he abandoned a law course at Glasgow University in 1877. After his father's death the following year he settled in London, where he met the artist John Pettie and, through him, William Quiller Orchardson and Tom Graham.

A short visit to Paris in 1882 had a profound effect on Guthrie. His sombre, low-toned paintings gave way to the sort of fresh colours and open brushwork he had seen in the work of Bastien-Lepage. By 1884 he was working in the village of Cockburnspath, accompanied in successive years by many friends, from Crawhall and Henry to Melville and Whitelaw Hamilton. In the early 1880s he painted *plein air* landscapes and figural subjects for the most part.

In 1885, after a cousin dissuaded him from abandoning painting altogether, Guthrie set out on a profitable career as a portraitist and became a prominent member of society. He was knighted in 1903 and served as PRSA from 1902 until his resignation in 1919. Abroad, his academic memberships included the Société Nationale des Beaux-Arts, Paris and the Bavarian Royal Academy, Munich. In 1920 he was made a Commander of Belgium's Order of the Crown.

George Henry trained at the Glasgow School of Art while working as a clerk. From 1881 he joined James Guthrie and E.A. Walton at Brig o'Turk and Rosneath, gradually becoming one of the leading Glasgow Boys. In the summer of 1883 he visited Eyemouth, near Cockburnspath. His square brushstrokes, impasto and pure colours betray Guthrie's influence. During the same period he spent the winters working in Macgregor's Glasgow studio. In 1885 he met E.A. Hornel, whose homes in Kirkcudbright and Glasgow he frequented. Henry's painting now moved away from the naturalism of Bastien-Lepage, and together with Hornel he developed a Symbolist art based on the decorative potential of colour, surface and pattern. Their work was most similar in 1888, and in 1890 and 1891 they collaborated on two large canvases. In 1893-94 Henry and Hornel visited Japan. They had recently been depicting young girls in nature; once they had been orientalised, such compositions lost much of their symbolic power and vision. By 1900 Henry's style had become almost slick. In 1902 he was elected RSA, but by 1908 he was living in London, where he became a member of the RA in 1920 and painted conventional landscapes and figural subjects.

Though born in Victoria, Australia, E.A. Hornel was brought up in Kirkcudbright, a town in southwest Scotland with which his family was connected. He trained first of all at the Trustees' Academy in Edinburgh, where his fellow students included D.Y. Cameron and James Pryde. Moving to Antwerp in 1883 he studied for two years at the Academy with Verlat. Returning to Kirkcudbright his friendship with George Henry from 1885, together with his awareness of Belgian art, helped foster a decorative style of painting that reached its peak in their joint canvases of 1890 and 1891. The Hague School paintings (especially those of Matthijs Maris) shown at the International Exhibitions in Edinburgh in 1886 and Glasgow in 1888 also shaped his art. In 1893-94 Hornel visited Japan with Henry. His oils from that date rank among his best in their amalgamation of Belgian Expressionism, decorative rhythm, rich colour and impasto. His later work, often depicting girls in wooded landscapes or on the seashore, was highly sentimental but popular. He travelled to Ceylon (Sri Lanka) in 1907 and in 1922 paid a return visit to Japan (and Burma). Hornel enjoyed the quiet country life of Kirkcudbright, where he preferred creating a Japanese garden at his eighteenth-century home to the bustle and bureaucracy of public life. In 1901 he even declined an ARSA.

William Kennedy
1859-1918

Sir John Lavery
1856-1941

William Kennedy was born in Hutchesontown, Glasgow. An orphan, he was raised by an elder brother. Kennedy studied at Paisley School of Art in 1875 and in Paris under Bouguereau and Fleury around 1880-85 and with Bastien-Lepage, Collin and Courtois. Kennedy's style was influenced by Corot, and his subject matter by Millet and the Hague School. He was elected a member of the Glasgow Art Club in 1884. The artist's importance within the Glasgow School can be traced to the late 1880s: when the Boys formed a society in 1887, they elected Kennedy president. At that time he was living in Cambuskenneth, near Stirling, where he would join Guthrie, Walton, Henry and Crawhall to paint. His friendship with these artists, and with Lavery, helped determine the course of his career. From 1900 Kennedy visited Berkshire where the rustic character of the area appealed to him. In 1912, for reasons of ill health, he went to live in Tangier, where Lavery already had a house.

In 1887 he met Whistler who inspired much of his work of the late 1880s, most notably his series of paintings of the 1888 Glasgow International Exhibition. He was commissioned to paint an official picture of the visit of Queen Victoria to the Exhibition. In 1890 he travelled to Morocco, where he met Crawhall and R.B. Cunninghame Graham. He settled in London in the early 1890s and set up a successful practice as a society portrait painter. As a portraitist Lavery enjoyed a brilliant career at home and abroad. He was knighted in 1918, elected RSA in 1896 and RA in 1921, and awarded honorary doctorates by the universities of Belfast and Dublin. In 1901 Italy awarded the artist the Order of the Crown, and in 1907 Belgium made him Chevalier of the Order of Leopold. Lavery exhibited widely as a member of the Secessions of Berlin, Munich and Vienna and of the Academies of Rome, Antwerp, Milan, Brussels and Stockholm.

John Lavery was brought up in Ireland on an Ulster farm but went to live with relatives in Saltcoats. In Glasgow he worked as a railway clerk and in a pawnbroker's shop, before being apprenticed to the Glasgow photographer and portrait painter J.B. MacNair. About 1876 Lavery enrolled in the Glasgow School of Art and in 1879 set himself up as a portraitist. His early paintings, dominated by costume pieces and portraits, showed no sign of any influence from France or Holland. Later that year his studio was destroyed by fire but, with the compensation money, he enrolled at Heatherley's Art School in London, returning to Glasgow the next year. In 1881 he was elected to Glasgow Art Club, whereupon he set off for Paris to study at the Académie Julian. After returning to Glasgow briefly in 1882, he was back in Paris that winter. In 1883 he discovered Grez-sur-Loing with William Kennedy, Thomas Millie Dow and Alexander Roche: that year a painting, *Les Deux Pecheurs,* was shown at the Salon. He returned to Grez the following summer, where he remained for a year; he might have stayed longer had not the Ecole des Beaux-Arts introduced an entrance exam that deterred foreign students.

In Glasgow, despite his enthusiasm for Guthrie's *To Pastures New,* shown in 1885 at the GIFA, Lavery adapted his style and subject matter to suit a middle-class market who were not particularly interested in his ruralist work.

James Pittendrigh Macgillivray
1856-1938

William York Macgregor
1855-1923

Charles Rennie Mackintosh
1868-1928

James Pittendrigh Macgillivray was born in Inverurie, Aberdeenshire. In his teens he moved to Edinburgh to study sculpture with William Brodie, and then from the age of twenty worked with the Glasgow sculptor James Mossman. Macgillivray was the only sculptor associated with the Glasgow Boys; he painted only a few pictures. Interested in Scottish national history and politics as much as art, he was also an amateur musician and a poet, the author of the anthologies *Pro Patria* and *Bog Myrtle and Peat Reek*. In the mid-1890s he moved back to Edinburgh where he spent the rest of his life. Besides sculpture he also contributed to the capital's artistic life by helping establish Edinburgh College of Art in 1906-08. Macgillivray had many artist friends in Scotland and the rest of Europe; indeed the Belgian sculptor Charles van der Stappen presented a bronze relief to the Glasgow Art Club in token of their friendship. He drew on his knowledge of artistic training in Brussels, Berlin and Paris in forming his proposals for Scottish education in the 1900s. His Glasgow School associates included Paterson, Henry and Hornel, and he was a leading contributor to both *The Scottish Art Review* (1888-89) in Glasgow and *The Evergreen* (1895-96) in Edinburgh.

From the 1890s Pittendrigh Macgillivray was Scotland's most celebrated and distinguished sculptor, who received many official and private commissions. In recognition of this he was appointed King's Sculptor in Ordinary for Scotland in 1921. Other distinctions included ARSA in 1892, RSA in 1901, and an honorary doctorate from Aberdeen University in 1909.

The son of a Glasgow shipbuilder, Macgregor was born in Finnart in Dunbartonshire. He studied under James Docharty in Glasgow and under Legros at the Slade School in London. Returning to Scotland Macgregor's friendship with James Paterson helped foster his aesthetics. He was elected to the Glasgow Art Club in 1881. In the early 1880s Macgregor's Glasgow studio at 134 Bath Street became a popular meeting place for artists. It was there that he advised them not to follow any school, as 'there are no schools in art'. His direct approach to the art of painting was in fact more important to art in Glasgow than his own work, earning him in early histories of the group the title of the 'father of the school'. His large canvas *The Vegetable Stall* of 1883-84 (National Gallery of Scotland) encapsulates his realist approach to art and is the work by which he is now remembered. In 1886 ill health forced him to leave Glasgow for Bridge of Allan in Stirlingshire, just as it prompted a visit to South Africa in 1888.

Macgregor exhibited and sold work in Munich in 1890. Though his painting never achieved the facility of that of the other Boys, nor the popularity accorded to Lavery or Guthrie, Macgregor was elected to the RSW in 1885 and was elected ARSA in 1898 and RSA in 1921.

Mackintosh was born in Glasgow, the son of a police superintendent. Apprenticed to the architect John Hutchison, he attended classes at the Glasgow School of Art. In 1889 he joined the practice of Honeyman & Keppie, where he met Herbert MacNair. At the School of Art he also met Margaret Macdonald (whom he was to marry in 1900) and her sister Frances. These four artists and architect-designers, whose work shared a symbolist identity, became a recognised group in the 1890s and were referred to as 'The Four'. They showed together at the Turin International Exhibition of Decorative Art in 1902.

At first Mackintosh designed architecture and furniture in accordance with the Arts and Crafts movement, but in the later 1890s his visual sensibilities developed dramatically. His work from this time not only showed an awareness of indigenous tradition and the organic principles of Arts and Crafts, but also began to embrace the positive values of Modernism. In the early 1900s his design became progressively less gothic (in the artistic and natural sense) and more fundamentally classical. In his mature work Mackintosh achieved a purity and intensity unsurpassed in British design.

In 1897 Mackintosh won the competition for a new building to house the Glasgow School of Art and received his first of many commissions from Catherine Cranston to design tea room interiors. In the decade 1895-1905 Mackintosh also executed a number of Glasgow public

buildings, including Martyrs' Public School (1895), Queen's Cross Church (1897) and Scotland Street School (1904). Between 1900 and 1905 he exhibited (e.g. Vienna 1900, Turin 1902, Moscow 1903, Berlin 1905) and was published abroad. It was also during these years that he designed and, together with Margaret, furnished his most important houses, including Windyhill in Kilmacolm (1900) for William Davidson, and Hill House in Helensburgh (1902) for Walter Blackie. He designed the second phase of the School of Art in 1906, but not long thereafter the commissions came to a halt. In 1913 Mackintosh finally resigned from his firm, now Honeyman, Keppie & Mackintosh. The Mackintoshes decided to move south, first to Walberswick in 1914 and the following year to London where they settled in Chelsea. When war made the practice of architecture impossible, Mackintosh turned to textile design, producing avant-garde work that was either organic or geometric but above all vigorous and colourful.

Mackintosh's last major architectural commission (1915) was to remodel the Northampton home of W.J. Bassett-Lowke. In 1923 the Mackintoshes closed their house in Chelsea and moved to the south of France. There Mackintosh painted a number of watercolour landscapes with a brilliant clarity of structure and colour. In 1927 he returned to London, and died there of cancer the following year.

Bessie MacNicol
1869-1904

Born in Glasgow, Bessie MacNicol was the twin daughter of a schoolmaster. From 1887 she studied at the Glasgow School of Art and in 1892 went to Paris to attend art classes at the Académie Colarossi. In 1893 she exhibited at the Royal Academy in London. After returning from Paris she showed at the GIFA from 1895 and the following year acquired a studio at 175 St Vincent Street. She soon became Glasgow's leading woman artist. In Glasgow and in Kirkcudbright, which she first visited in 1896, she became part of a coterie of Glasgow artists including Hornel - whose portrait she painted - and George Henry, W.S. MacGeorge, David Gauld and John Keppie. From that year she exhibited at home and abroad, especially at the Munich Secession. MacNicol started painting her most important pictures at this point. Many of these are studies of young women and show her interest in sunlight, in costume and, not least, in surface texture.

In 1899 MacNicol married Alexander Frew, a physician who had become a full-time painter. In Glasgow they moved into a house in Hillhead, where D.Y. Cameron had previously lived. She died in childbirth at the early age of thirty-four.

Arthur Melville
1855-1904

Born at Loanhead-of-Guthrie in Angus, Arthur Melville moved with his family to East Linton in East Lothian. Working as a clerk in the town of Dalkeith he studied part-time, then full-time, under James Campbell Noble at the Trustees' Academy in Edinburgh. In 1878 he went to live in Paris where, instead of training in an atelier, he studied the contemporary work of the Impressionists. He also visited Grez-sur-Loing, where he began to experiment with the transparent qualities of watercolour. The pictures he painted in 1879 still showed the influence of both Corot and Bastien-Lepage - the restrained palette, for instance, and the pearly quality of the light - but in the autumn of 1880 Melville journeyed to the Middle East, visiting Cairo, Istanbul, Karachi and Baghdad. From this date his colours brightened in an attempt to capture the effect of hot, reflected sunlight. He first visited Cockburnspath in 1884. In 1886 and 1889 he went to France with James Guthrie and E.A. Walton, and then to Spain and North Africa in 1890 and again in the following two years. He visited Venice in 1894.

After marrying Ethel Croall in 1899 Melville settled in Whitley, Surrey, where he began experimenting with oils. He died after contracting typhoid on a visit to Spain in 1904.

James Stuart Park
1862-1933

James Park was born in Kidderminster, the son of an Ayrshire carpet designer. He adapted his mother's maiden name of Stewart, and added it to his own. Little is known about Park's early life, except that he studied in Glasgow and in Paris under Lefèvre, Boulanger and Cormon. After returning to Glasgow he became a member of the Glasgow Art Club in 1892. Unlike most artists of the Glasgow school he remained in the west of Scotland his entire professional life.
Now remembered primarily for a series of oil paintings of yellow, pink or red roses which he executed in 1889-1990, Park also produced a series of flower studies against dark backgrounds not long afterwards, many of which were exhibited at the McLellan Galleries. Like David Gauld and George Henry he is also responsible for a series of young girls surrounded by flowers which he painted in the early 1890s.

James Paterson
1854-1932

The son of a cotton manufacturer, James Paterson was born in Hillhead, Glasgow. He trained at the Glasgow School of Art and studied watercolour with A.D. Robertson in about 1874-76. In 1877 Paterson renewed his friendship with W.Y. Macgregor, whom he had known at school. In Paris he worked with Jacquesson de la Chevreuse in 1877-79, and Jean Paul Laurens in 1879-83. He was elected a member of the Glasgow Art Club in 1882. After marrying Eliza Ferguson in 1884 he settled in Moniaive, Dumfriesshire. Though soon immersed in the country life of southwest Scotland, Paterson maintained close ties with Glasgow; he helped establish *The Scottish Art Review* in 1888, and was responsible for hanging the 1890 GIFA exhibition. He exhibited oils and watercolours widely, including Glasgow, Edinburgh and London, and recame RSW in 1885 (PRSW in 1922-32), RWS in 1908 and a NEAC member in 1887. In 1896 he was elected ARSA and in 1910 RSA. In 1890 he won a gold medal at the Munich Secession for his painting *Passing Storm*. In 1906 Paterson moved to Edinburgh where he helped establish the exhibiting group the Society of Eight in 1912.

John Quinton Pringle
1864-1925

John Quinton Pringle was born in the east end of Glasgow. He grew up at Langbank, near Greenock, where his father was the stationmaster. In 1874 the family moved back to Glasgow. Pringle was apprenticed to an optician and ultimately became a highly skilled craftsman. He was awarded an evening school bursary to Glasgow School of Art where his peers included Muirhead Bone, D.Y. Cameron and Mackintosh. In 1896 he went into business as an optician and electrician in the Saltmarket and, aside from the 1899-1900 session, ceased to attend the School. In the evenings he started painting miniatures, which were fashionable once again, and won a number of important commissions. His interest in Impressionism also influenced his painting style, characterised by tiny fragments of pure colour alongside one another.In 1910 Pringle visited Caudebec in Normandy. The following year his sister, who had assisted in the shop, died suddenly and his painting output sharply declined. Between Caudebec and a visit to the Shetland Isles in 1921 he produced no oils. In 1922 an exhibition of his work was mounted at the Glasgow School of Art.

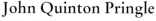

Robert Macaulay Stevenson
1854-1952

Macaulay Stevenson was born in Glasgow, where he attended the School of Art part-time. His early work was Naturalist but, by the late 1880s, his work was profoundly influenced by Corot's imaginative treatment and technique. A theorist of the Glasgow School and more of a critic than an artist of great originality, he developed the theory of 'Constructive Idealism', according to which art's purpose is to capture the *genius loci,* the essential spirit of a place. He preferred working from memory to working from nature, however; though the *'colours fade, the aspect changes, the leaves die, the picture as it was in Nature ceases to be',* nevertheless *'the recollection remains, and that memory I transcribe on to canvas. And since the remembrance stays with us, while the actuality fades and perishes, is not the memory that does not perish the essential human fact, the really living part?'*
A member of the Glasgow Art Club from 1886, Macaulay Stevenson served as president in 1898-99. He was a member of the Munich Secession, which awarded him a gold medal in 1893; the following year he received a diploma from the Barcelona Academy. His moonlit landscapes were especially popular in Germany, Spain and the United States. Stevenson lived in France from 1910 and in Kirkcudbright between 1932 and 1951. The last survivor of the Glasgow School, he died at his former home in Milngavie, north of Glasgow, aged ninety-eight.

Edward Arthur Walton
1860-1922

E.A. Walton came from a talented artistic family of twelve children, including Helen, Hannah and George Walton. Born in Renfrewshire, he was trained at Düsseldorf Academy and the Glasgow School of Art. In 1878 he met James Guthrie who, with Joseph Crawhall, was to be a lifelong friend and painting colleague: Walton's brother Richard married Crawhall's sister. In 1879 Guthrie, Walton and Crawhall painted at Rosneath on the Clyde and, also with Guthrie, Walton first visited Brig o'Turk in 1880. In contrast to Lavery, Walton was instinctively a landscape painter, and travelled to Crowland, Lincolnshire (with Crawhall and Guthrie) in 1882. The following year they painted for the first time at Cockburnspath in Berwickshire, where they were joined in subsequent years by Henry, Melville and Corson Morton. In 1886 Walton set up a studio at Cambuskenneth. His travels took him to Paris with Melville in 1889. In 1893 he settled in London's Cheyne Walk, attracted by the Whistler circle and the NEAC, with whom he had shown from 1887. Contact with his neighbour Whistler broadened his approach to watercolour and encouraged experiment with transparent washes and decorative understatement. In 1904 he returned to Scotland and settled in Edinburgh, where he was elected RSA the following year. His travels were not over, however, for he visited Algiers and Spain with Guthrie in 1907, and Brussels and Ghent in 1913. Elected RSW already in 1885, he served as PRSW in 1915-22.

1

Jules Bastien-Lepage
(1848-1884)
Pauvre Fauvette
1881
oil on canvas
162.5 x 125.7 cm
signed, dated and inscribed
Damvillers

Glasgow Museums and Art Galleries 1323

In many ways it is surprising that
no work by Bastien-Lepage, the
artist who most influenced the
Naturalist painting style of the
Glasgow Boys, entered the
Glasgow municipal collection
before 1913. However the
present canvas was purchased the
same year that the National
Gallery of Scotland in Edinburgh
bought the oil *Pas Mèche* (1882),
which had been shown at the
1888 Glasgow International
Exhibition and received wide, if
not always favourable, publicity.

Collections
James Staats Forbes, London; George
McCulloch; his sale, Christie's, 23 May
1913, lot 9

Exhibitions
1882   United Arts Gallery, London
        (165)
1909-10 *The Collection of the late
        George McCulloch*, Royal
        Academy, London (27)
1911   Royal Glasgow Institute of Fine
        Arts Jubilee Exhibition (94)
1917   Paisley Art Institute
1927   Walker Art Gallery, Liverpool
1940   *Narrative Paintings*, Glasgow
        Museums and Art Galleries
        (165)
1958   Greenock Art Gallery Opening
        Exhibition (1)
1972   *Young Bert*, Nottingham Castle
        Museum (123)
1979   *Post-Impressionism: Cross-
        currents in European Painting*,
        Royal Academy, London (10)
1981   *Peasantries*, Newcastle Festival
        Exhibition (39)

2
Paul Cézanne
(1839-1906)
Overturned Basket of Fruit
c. 1877
oil on canvas
16 x 32.2 cm

Glasgow Museums and Art Galleries 2382

Through the bequest of the shipowner William McInnes in 1944, Glasgow Art Gallery acquired a number of paintings previously handled by Alexander Reid. They included this Cézanne still life, the first Van Gogh handled by Reid (surprisingly late, in the 1920s), a Degas pastel and paintings by the Scottish artist Leslie Hunter, in whom Reid had begun to deal towards the end of his career. The directness with which Cézanne approached his subjects was to have particular appeal for the Scottish Colourists: the painters J.D. Fergusson, S.J. Peploe, F.C.B. Cadell and Leslie Hunter. Like the Glasgow Boys before them, the Colourists were to seek a European identity.

Collections
Ambroise Vollard, Paris; C. Hoogendijk, Amsterdam; Paul Rosenberg; Charles Ruloz, Paris; Alex. Reid, Glasgow; sold by Reid to William McInnes, by whom bequeathed 1944

Exhibitions
1921   *Paintings by the great French Impressionists from the collection of Paul Rosenberg of Paris*, Wildenstein, New York (31)
1924   *Important pictures by 19th century French Masters*, Reid & Lefèvre, London
1925   Alex. Reid Exhibition, Glasgow
1943   *The Spirit of France*, Glasgow Museums & Art Galleries (52)
1954   *Cézanne*, Tate Gallery, London (17)
1954   Kunstnerforbundet, Oslo
1954/55 Helsinki Art Gallery
1974   *Cézanne*, Museum of Western Art, Tokyo (18)
1980   *Paintings from Glasgow Art Gallery*, Wildenstein, London (4: illus. p.27)

Literature
Lionello Venturi, *Cézanne, son art, son oeuvre*, Paris 1936, no. 211.
The Burlington Magazine 98 (1956), p. 88.
Apollo 57 (1953), p. 40.
The Scottish Art Review 7, no. 3 (1960), (illus. p. 16).
Alfonso Gatto, *L'Opera completa di Cézanne*, Milan 1970.

3
Jean Baptiste Camille Corot
(1796-1875)
The Woodcutter
1865-70
oil on canvas
49.8 x 64.8 cm
signed

Glasgow Museums and Art Galleries 1115

Works by Corot and Daubigny were exhibited at the Glasgow Institute in 1872. In 1878 a loan exhibition of works of both the Hague and Barbizon Schools was held in the Corporation of Glasgow's Art Galleries. Corot's atmospheric work was immensely popular with both the collectors - such as James Donald and James Reid of Auchterarder - and the painters of the Glasgow School.

Collections
James Donald; Donald Bequest, 1905

Exhibitions
1960   *Corot*, Art Institute of Chicago
1981   *Peasantries*, Newcastle Festival
        Exhibition (1: illus.)

4
Jozef Israëls
(1824-1911)
The Frugal Meal
c. 1870-75
oil on canvas
89 x 138.7 cm

Glasgow Museums and Art Galleries 737

In the 1870s work by the Hague School, including Jacob Maris, Anton Mauve and Jozef Israëls, was shown at the Glasgow Institute. Israëls's subjects held particular appeal for collectors interested in painting that had no social commentary but echoed recent Scottish genre painting. A watercolour study is preserved in the Rijksmuseum Amsterdam (1934.2926-9). The painting was etched by Ferdinand Leenhoff and Leopold Loewenstam.

Collections
John McGavin (d. 1881), Glasgow (by 1876); James Reid of Auchterarder (by 1888); presented by his sons to Glasgow Corporation, 1896

Exhibitions
1876   Paris Salon (1073)
1877   GIFA (266)
1888   Glasgow International Exhibition (638)
1900   RSA, Edinburgh (179)
1912   Victoria Art Gallery, Dundee (265)
1913   Smith Institute, Stirling
1915   Dick Institute, Kilmarnock
1940   *Narrative Paintings,* Glasgow Museums and Art Galleries (21: illus.)
1949   Ben Uri Gallery, London (3)
1977   RGIFA (62)

Literature
L'Art 5 (1876), p. 154; 6 (1876), p. 76.
Kunstkroniek (1886) (illus. opposite p. 84).
W.E. Henley, *A Century of Artists,* Glasgow 1889, p. 90.
The Magazine of Art (1894), p. 156 (illus. p. 153).
E. Pinnington, *G.P. Chalmers,* Glasgow 1896, pp. 267, 274.
E. Pinnington, *The Art Collection [...] of Glasgow,* Glasgow 1898, p. 22 (illus.).
A. Bell, *Representative Painters of the Nineteenth Century,* London 1899 (illus. opposite p. 176).
J.E. Phythian, *Israëls,* London 1912 (illus. opposite p. 20).
M. Eisler, *Israëls,* London 1924 (pl. XXXIII).
H.E. van Gelder, *Israëls* (Palet Serie), Amsterdam 1947, p. 38 (illus. p. 33).

5
Jean François Millet
(1814-1875)
Going to Work
1850-51
oil on canvas
55.5 x 46 cm

Glasgow Museums and Art Galleries 1111

For over a century this has been
one of the most renowned
French paintings in Scotland. It
was shown at both the 1886
Edinburgh International
Exhibition and the 1888 Glasgow
International Exhibition, lent by
James Donald. A variant was
executed for Sensier in 1851-53
and is now in the Cincinnati Art
Museum. The figures have a
timeless quality and could belong
equally to the sixteenth or the
nineteenth century. This no
doubt was part of its appeal to a
collector who was less interested
in social commentary than in an
evocation of simple rusticity.

Collections
Millet's dealer, Collet; Justice C. Day;
sold 24 March 1882 to Boussod, Valadon
et Cie, sold (same day) to James Donald;
Donald Bequest, 1905

Exhibitions
1883   *Institute of the Fine Arts*,
        Glasgow (38)
1886   Edinburgh International
        Exhibition (French and Dutch
        Loan Collection: 1138)
1888   Glasgow International
        Exhibition (667)
1889   *Flemish and Dutch
        Romanticists*, Dowdeswell
        Galleries, London (81)
1898   Guildhall, London (115)
1901   Glasgow International
        Exhibition (1300)
1925   *Inaugural Exhibition*, Kirkcaldy
        Museums & Art Gallery (16)
1925   *Centenary Exhibition*, Castle
        Museum, Norwich (34)
1932   *Exhibition of French Art*, Royal
        Academy, London and
        Manchester (347)
1943   *The Spirit of France*, Glasgow
        Museums & Art Galleries (24)
1944   *A Century of French Art*,
        National Gallery of Scotland,
        Edinburgh (141)
1950   *The School of 1830 in France*,
        Wildenstein, London (51)
1962   *Primitives to Picasso*, Royal
        Academy, London (214)
1969   *J.F. Millet*, Wildenstein, London
        (26)
1974   *Impressionism*, Royal Academy,
        London (46)
1980   *Paintings from Glasgow Art
        Gallery*, Wildenstein, London
        (18; illus. p.26)
1991   *Man and Work in XIXth
        Century Painting*, Biblioteca
        Apostolica Vaticana, Rome

Literature
A Sensier, *J.F. Millet*, London 1881, p. 90.
*Memorial Catalogue of French and Dutch
Loan Collections*, Edinburgh 1888, p. 54,
no. 78.
W.E. Henley, *A Century of Artists*,
Glasgow 1889, p. 125.
Croal Thomson, *The Barbizon School of
Painters*, London 1891, p. 227.
Percy Bates, *Art at the Glasgow
Exhibition, 1901*, London 1901, p. 74
(illus. p. 80).
D.S. MacColl, *Nineteenth Century Art*,
Glasgow 1902, p. 88 (illus.).
Art Journal (1905), p. 190 (illus.).
L. Delteil, *Peintre-Graveur*, Paris 1906,
vol. 1, no. 19.
The Studio 39 (1907), p. 198.
E. Moreau-Nelaton, *Millet raconté par
lui-meme*, Paris 1921, p. 89.
The Scottish Art Review 1 (1947), no. 4, p.
22 (illus.).
Robert Herbert, *Millet reconsidered in
Museum Studies*, Art Institute of Chicago
1966, p. 60.
Alan Bowness (ed.), *The Book of Art*, vol.
7, *Impressionists and post-Impressionists*,
p. 69 (illus.).
T.J. Clark, *The Absolute Bourgeois*,
London 1973, p. 97, illus. p. 78.
Griselda Pollock, *Millet*, London 1977, p.
45 (illus.).

Waldemar Januszczak, *Techniques of the
World's Great Painters*, London 1980, pp.
88 - 91 (illus.).
Laura Wortley, *British Impressionism*,
London 1988 (illus. p. 81).
*Glasgow Art Gallery & Museum - the
Building & the Collections*, Glasgow
1987, p. 129 (illus. p. 131).

6
Camille Jacob Pissarro
(1830-1903)
The Tuileries Gardens
1900
oil on canvas
73.6 x 92.3 cm
signed and dated

Glasgow Museums & Art Galleries 2811

Alexander Reid acquired his first Pissarro in 1889. He continued to sell his work until he retired in 1926, upon the merger of his gallery with the Lefèvre Gallery in London. Sir John Richmond was one of Reid's later clients, whose collection the dealer largely shaped; now divided between the Glasgow Art Gallery and the National Gallery of Scotland, the collection comprised French and Scottish paintings for the most part, including pictures by Boudin, Monticelli, Monet and Le Sidaner.

There are at least fourteen versions of the present canvas in existence (see Pissarro & Venturi, nos. 1123-36).

Collections
Alexander Reid; sold 1911 to Sir John Richmond, by whom presented 1948

Exhibitions
1943   *The Spirit of France*, Glasgow Museums and Art Galleries (26)
1944   *A Century of French Art*, National Galleries of Scotland, Edinburgh (187)
1949   123rd Annual Exhibition, Royal Scottish Academy, Edinburgh (276)
1949   *Landscape in French Art*, Royal Academy, London (279)
1967   *A Man of Influence*, Alexander Reid, 1854-1928, Scottish Arts Council Gallery, Glasgow (36)
1968   *Boudin to Picasso*, Royal Scottish Academy, Edinburgh (15)
1980-81 *Pissarro*, Hayward Gallery, London; Grand Palais, Paris; Museum of Fine Arts, Boston (85)

Literature
L.R. Pissarro & L. Venturi, *Camille Pissarro, son art, son oeuvre,* Paris 1939, no. 1133.
The Scottish Art Review 4 (1953), no. 3 (illus. p. 15).
The Scottish Art Review 6 (1957), no. 3 (illus. p. 2).

7
Sir George Reid
(1841-1913)
James Reid of Auchterarder
c. 1888-92
oil on canvas
144.8 x 97.9 cm
signed

Glasgow Museums and Art Galleries 760

Two west coast collectors helped shape Glasgow Art Gallery's modern collection in the beginning: James Donald and James Reid of Auchterarder. Donald bequeathed no fewer than forty-two pictures, from Corot, Daubigny and Millet to Monticelli and Rousseau. James Reid amassed a personal fortune as director of Neilson, Reid & Co., a Glasgow firm of locomotive engineers. His select collection included masterpieces of French and Dutch art, such as Corot's *Souvenir d'Italie* (1873), a major painting previously owned by the entrepreneurial Aberdeen collector, John Forbes White.

Collections
James Reid of Auchterarder; presented to Glasgow Museums by his sons in 1897

Literature
M. Nicholson and M. O'Neill, *Glasgow, Locomotive to the World*, Glasgow 1987, (illus. p. 7).

Collections
Mme J. van Gogh-Bonger; V.W. van Gogh (son of Theo van Gogh), Amsterdam; A.J. McNeill Reid (son of the sitter); Graham Reid (son of A.J. McNeill Reid); purchased by Glasgow Museums and Art Galleries with the aid of a special Government grant, the NA-CF and donations from a public appeal, 1974

Exhibitions
1914	Paul Cassirer, Berlin (36)
1930	*Renoir and the Post-Impressionists,* Lefèvre Gallery, London (14)
1930	*XIX and XX century French Paintings,* Alexander Reid & Lefèvre, Glasgow (20)
1932	*Vincent van Gogh,* City Art Gallery, Manchester (16)
1934	Royal Scottish Academy, Edinburgh (352)
1939/40	The Art Galleries of Melbourne, Adelaide and Sydney, Australia
1947	*The Nineteenth Century French Masters,* Lefèvre Gallery, Tate Gallery, London and tour (46)
1947-48	*Vincent van Gogh,* ACGB (26)
1951	*Géricault to Renoir,* Lefèvre Gallery, London (36)
1963	*The French Impressionists and some of their contemporaries,* Wildenstein, London (70)
1964	*Pictures to live with,* GAGM (144)
1967	*A Man of Influence: Alex. Reid 1854-1928,* Scottish Arts Council Gallery, Glasgow (41)
1974	*Important XIX and XX Century Paintings and Drawings,* Lefèvre Gallery, London (17)
1974	*25 Glorious Years,* Art Gallery and Museum, Glasgow (113)
1980	*Paintings from Glasgow Art Gallery,* Wildenstein, Glasgow
1988	*Van Gogh à Paris,* Musée d'Orsay, Paris (38)
1990	*Vincent van Gogh,* Rijksmuseum Vincent van Gogh, Amsterdam (26)
1990-91	*The Age of Van Gogh,* Glasgow Museums and Art Galleries
1991	*Saved for Scotland,* National Gallery of Scotland, Edinburgh (41)

8
Vincent Willem van Gogh
(1853-1890)
Portrait of Alexander Reid
1887
oil on board
42 x 33 cm
signed

Glasgow Museums and Art Galleries 3315

In 1887 James Reid, proprietor of a firm of Glasgow carvers and gilders, sent his son, Alexander, to Paris to join the dealers Boussod and Valadon. Though Reid was in Paris for only a few months, the experience was a revelation. Through the firm, a branch of which was run by Theo van Gogh, he not only became acquainted with the latest French art but also met a number of artists personally, including Toulouse-Lautrec and Theo's brother, Vincent. The visit marked the beginning of Reid's career as a dealer in French art.

In 1887 Van Gogh painted two portraits of Reid, the only British citizen known to have sat for him. The other portrait, a full-length seated study of Reid, may predate the present one by several months; it now belongs to a private American collection. Painter and sitter bore a distinct physical resemblance to one another, as the Scottish artist, A.S. Hartrick, remarked in his memoirs, *A Painter's Pilgrimage Through Fifty Years* (1939).

Literature
T.J. Honeyman, 'Van Gogh: A link with Glasgow', *The Scottish Art Review* 2 (1948), no. 2, pp. 16 - 20.
Ronald Pickvance, *A Man of Influence: Alexander Reid 1854-1928,* Edinburgh 1968, pp. 7 - 8.
J.-B. de la Faille, *The Works of Vincent van Gogh: His Paintings and Drawings,* Amsterdam 1970 (F343: illus.).
Jan Hulsker, *The Complete Van Gogh,* Oxford 1980, cat. no. 1250, p. 278 (illus.).
Richard Marks, *Sir William Burrell,* Glasgow Art Gallery, 1982, p. 12 (illus. p. 13, fig. 6).
Richard Marks, *Burrell: Portrait of a Collector,* Glasgow 1983, pp. 62 - 64 (illus. p. 63).

9
Sir David Muirhead Bone

Dry Dock
1899
etching and drypoint on paper
23.7 x 18.7 cm
signed and dated

Glasgow Museums and Art Galleries
21-26e

The print was an illustration to
Bone's book *Etchings of Glasgow*
(1899).

Collections
L.G. Pearson; purchased by Glasgow Art
Gallery and Museums, 1921

10
Sir David Young Cameron

Tintoretto's House, Venice
1894
etching on paper
24 x 11.5 cm
signed and dated

Glasgow Museums and Art Galleries
20-6ha

Collections
John Innes; presented by him to Glasgow
Museums, 1920

11
Joseph Crawhall

Landscape with Cattle
c. 1883-85
oil on canvas
43 x 57.8 cm
signed

Glasgow Museums and Art Galleries 3042

Landscape with Cattle shows
how clearly the Glasgow Boys
were influenced by their French
and Dutch contemporaries. Both
the compositional elements and
the static subject recall the Hague
School, especially Jacob Maris
and Anton Mauve, whose work
hung in the Glasgow Institute
and who were popular with both
collectors and dealers. The square
brushstrokes, however, evince
Crawhall's awareness of Bastien-
Lepage. The artist's palette
remained restricted (if brighter)
and his forms continued to
overlap long after watercolour
became his primary medium.

Collections
Mrs I.G. Balharry

Exhibitions
1968   *Glasgow Boys* (27)
1973   *Scottish Painting 1880-1930,*
        Glasgow Museums & Art
        Galleries (4: illus.)
1974   *Schottische Malerei 1880-1930,*
        Kunsthaus, Hamburg (4: illus.)
1981-82 *Sir James Guthrie and the
        Scottish Realists,* The Fine Art
        Society, Glasgow and London
        (51)
1990   *Joseph Crawhall,* Glasgow
        Museums and Art Galleries

Literature
Billcliffe, *The Glasgow Boys,* pp. 124-126
(illus. p. 125, pl. 114).
Vivien Hamilton, *Joseph Crawhall (1861-
1913): One of the Glasgow Boys,* London
1990, pp. 28-30 (illus. p. 23).

Joseph Crawhall

The Byre
c. 1885
watercolour on paper
34.2 x 32.5 cm
signed

Glasgow Museums and Art Galleries 2487

In 1884 Crawhall met Arthur Melville, who went to work at Cockburnspath that summer. The meeting may have inspired Crawhall and Walton to experiment with watercolour. Crawhall ultimately abandoned oils in favour of watercolour and gouache.

The Byre illustrates the development of the artist's watercolour technique. In his earlier watercolours he covered the paper entirely; in this case, however, where detail is suggested rather than described, Crawhall has used the support for colour as much as the paint, just as he did in his gouache sketches on linen.

Collections
John Keppie; bequeathed by him in 1945

Exhibitions
1985   *Camels, Cobwebs and Honeysuckles - A Brush with Nature: Edwin Alexander and Joseph Crawhall*, Edinburgh and London (10)
1990   *Joseph Crawhall*, Glasgow Museums and Art Galleries

Literature
Vivien Hamilton, *Joseph Crawhall (1861-1913): One of the Glasgow Boys,* London 1990, p. 38 (illus. p. 29).

13
Joseph Crawhall

Lady on Horseback
c. 1887-88
pen and watercolour on paper
18.1 x 18 cm
signed

Glasgow Museums and Art Galleries 2325

Collections
Hugh Locke Anderson Jr., Helensburgh;
bequeathed by him in 1943

Exhibitions
1944   *The Glasgow School*, Glasgow
        Museums and Art Galleries (44)
1986   *Town and Country - The Social
        Scene in Scotland 1850-1920*,
        Hunterian Art Gallery,
        University of Glasgow (67)

Literature
Adrian Bury, *Joseph Crawhall: The Man
and the Artist*, London 1958, p. 266.

14
Joseph Crawhall

Horse and Cart with a Lady
c. 1887-88
gouache on linen
22.2 x 29.9 cm
signed

Glasgow Museums and Art Galleries 2327

Collections
Hugh Locke Anderson Jr., Helensburgh;
bequeathed by him 1943

Exhibitions
1944   *The Glasgow School*, Glasgow
         Museums and Art Galleries, (46)
1973   *Scottish Painting 1880-1930*,
         Glasgow Museums and Art
         Galleries (6)
1974   *Schottische Malerei 1880-1930*,
         Kunsthaus, Hamburg (6)
1986   *Academics and Revolutionaries*,
         Glasgow Museums and Art
         Galleries

1990   *Joseph Crawhall*, Glasgow
         Museums and Art Galleries

Literature
Vivien Hamilton, *Joseph Crawhall (1861-
1913): One of the Glasgow Boys*, London
1990 (illus. p. 150).

15
Thomas Millie Dow

The Hudson River
1884
oil on canvas
123.2 x 97.8 cm
signed with initials

Glasgow Museums and Art Galleries 1739

Collections
William McLean; bequeathed to Glasgow
Museums by William McLean's Trust,
1928

Exhibitions
1888   Glasgow International
        Exhibition (173)
1892   Walker Art Gallery, Liverpool
1939   *Scottish Art*, Royal Academy,
        London
1968   *Glasgow Boys* (37)
1970   *The Glasgow School of Painting*,
        The Fine Art Society, London
        (5)
1973   *Scottish Painting, 1880-1930*,
        Glasgow Museums and Art
        Galleries (7)
1974   *Schottische Malerei, 1880-1930*,
        Kunsthaus, Hamburg (7)

Literature
William Hardie, *Scottish Painting 1837-
1939*, London 1976, p. 79.
Billcliffe, *The Glasgow Boys*, p. 81 (illus.
p. 86, pl. 75).

16
David Gauld

Portrait Head
c. 1893
oil on canvas
50.8 x 40.6 cm
signed

Glasgow Museums and Art Galleries 2802

In 1893, the year he married,
Gauld produced a number of
portrait heads, some of which
may represent his wife.
Following a series of Realist
landscapes, these paintings mark
a return to his decorative style of
the late 1880s.

Collections
Sir John Richmond; presented by him to
Glasgow Museums in 1948

Exhibitions
1973   *Scottish Painting 1880-1930,*
        Glasgow Museums and Art
        Galleries (12)
1974   *Schottische Malerei 1880-1930,*
        Kunsthaus, Hamburg (12)

17
Maurice Greiffenhagen

Fra Newbery
1913
oil on canvas
132.1 x 102.2 cm
signed and dated

Glasgow Museums and Art Galleries 2154

For a biographical note on Francis ('Fra')
Newbery, see pages 120-1.

Collections
The sitter; presented by him in 1940

Exhibitions
1947   Royal Scottish Academy Annual
        Exhibition
1990   Glasgow

Literature
William Buchanan (ed.), *Mackintosh's
Masterwork: The Glasgow School of Art*,
Glasgow 1989, p. 130 (illus.).
Burkhauser, *Glasgow Girls,* 1990, p. 63
(illus. fig. 67).

18
Sir James Guthrie

Two studies: Sketching from Nature
1878
pen and ink on paper
18.1 x 11.4 cm
inscribed with title
the paper bears the postmark
Glasgow/May 14/78

Glasgow Museums and Art Galleries
33.12e

Collections
Mr Lamont; presented by him to
Glasgow Museums in 1933

Exhibitions
1986   *Town and Country - The Social*
        Scene in Scotland 1850-1920,
        Hunterian Art Gallery, Glasgow
        (79: illus.)
1986   *Academics and Revolutionaries,*
        Glasgow Museums and Art
        Galleries

19
Sir James Guthrie

When Autumn Winds So Softly Breathe
c. 1883
pen and ink on paper
15.9 x 9.8 cm
inscribed with title

Glasgow Museums and Art Galleries
33-12c

The drawing is part of a letter
dated Oct. 25th. The paper bears
the postmark *Cockburnspath/Oct*
26/83 (?).

Collections
Mr Lamont; presented by him to
Glasgow Museums in 1933

Literature:
Billcliffe, *The Glasgow Boys* (illus. p. 108,
pl. 96).

20
Sir James Guthrie

Hard at It
1883
oil on canvas
31.1 x 46.0 cm
signed and dated

Glasgow Museums and Art Galleries 3248

Possibly a self-portrait of Guthrie at work, this finished oil sketch differs in colour from the artist's other early, predominantly dark, Cockburnspath paintings. The blue sky is more reminiscent of work he had recently produced at Crowland in Lincolnshire. The paint is applied in broad sweeping strokes of blues, mauves, ochres and greens with much greater fluency than in the late 1870s and early 1880s.

Collections
F.C. Gardiner; The Fine Art Society, London

Exhibitions
1968   *Glasgow Boys* (148)
1973   *Scottish Painting 1880-1930,* Glasgow Museums and Art Galleries (13)
1974   *Schottische Malerei 1880-1930,* Kunsthaus, Hamburg (13)
1977   *25 Glorious Years,* Glasgow Museums and Art Galleries (74)
1981-82 *Sir James Guthrie and the Scottish Realists,* The Fine Art Society, Glasgow and London (13)
1983   *Landscape in Britain 1850-1950,* ACGB, Hayward Gallery, London and tour (88)
1990   Glasgow

Literature
David Martin, *The Glasgow School of Painting,* London 1897, pp. 32 - 33 (illus. 1976 reprint).
David and Francina Irwin, *Scottish Painters at Home and Abroad 1700-1900,* London 1975, p. 384, pl. 188.
William Hardie, *Scottish Painting 1837-1939,* London 1976, p. 76.
Billcliffe, *The Glasgow Boys,* pp. 105-109 (illus. p. 109, pl. 98).

21
Sir James Guthrie

Old Willie - a Village Worthy
1886
oil on canvas
60.8 x 50.8 cm
signed, dated and inscribed
Kirkcudbright

Glasgow Museums and Art Galleries 3314

A painting entitled *A Village
Worthy* by Guthrie was lent to
the Glasgow East End Industrial
Exhibition in 1903-04 (204) by
William Young RSW.

Collections
The Fine Art Society, Edinburgh

Exhibitions
1864   Royal Scottish Academy (275: as
        Study)
1979   *Glasgow 1900,* The Fine Art
        Society, Glasgow
1981-82 *Sir James Guthrie and the
        Scottish Realists,* The Fine Art
        Society, Glasgow and London

Literature
James L. Caw, *Sir James Guthrie,*
London 1932, p. 43.
Billcliffe, *The Glasgow Boys,* pp. 188-192,
198 (illus. pp. 187, pl. 179).

22
George Henry

Brig o'Turk
1882
oil on canvas
30.5 x 45.1 cm
signed and dated

Glasgow Museums and Art Galleries 3337

E.A. Walton and James Guthrie
first visited Brig o'Turk, a village
in the Trossach hills north of
Glasgow, in 1880. Henry started
joining them there the following
summer. During this first visit he
assimilated his friends' thematic
ideals and techniques, especially
their interest in rural life and
their free handling of oil paint
and low-key tonality.

Collections
The Fine Art Society; presented by the
Society in 1977

Literature
Billcliffe, *The Glasgow Boys,* p. 53 (illus.
p. 52, pl. 43).

23
George Henry

Landscape
1882
watercolour on paper
32.4 x 48.2 cm
signed and dated

Glasgow Museums and Art Galleries 69-2a

This landscape contrasts
markedly with the misty
Highland glens and rugged
mountain scenery that still
figured prominently in art
academy exhibitions.

24
George Henry

The Girl in White
1886
watercolour on paper
60.3 x 37 cm
signed and dated

Glasgow Museums and Art Galleries 2104

Henry regularly visited Hornel at
his home in Kirkcudbright,
Galloway, from the summer of
1885. The work the two artists
produced in the later 1880s
diverged from that of the other
Glasgow Boys: no longer
concerned with rustic
Naturalism, they began
experimenting with decorative
effects and moving towards a
Symbolist intensity of colour and
pattern. A recurrent theme
between approximately 1887 and
1893 - before they visited Japan -
was young women or girls in
thickly wooded landscapes.
Henry's approach to the present
watercolour was still Realist, but
the placement of a female figure
in wooded undergrowth
anticipated future developments.

Collections
George Gilchrist Paterson; Betty
Paterson; presented by Miss Betty
Paterson in 1938

Exhibitions
1981-82 *Sir James Guthrie and the
Scottish Realists*, The Fine Art
Society, Glasgow and London
(57)
1987 *Academics and Revolutionaries*,
Glasgow Museums and Art
Galleries

Literature
Julian Halsby, *Scottish Watercolours
1740-1940*, London 1986, p. 142 (illus.
p. 142).
Billcliffe, *The Glasgow Boys*, p. 196 (illus.
p. 197, pl. 188).

George Henry

Theresa
1888
watercolour on paper
44 x 34 cm
signed, dated and inscribed
Theresa

Glasgow Museums and Art Galleries 66-5

Exhibitions
1981-82 *Sir James Guthrie and the*
            Scottish Realists, The Fine Art
            Society, Glasgow and London
            (58)

26
George Henry

Autumn
1888
oil on canvas
45.7 x 38.1 cm
signed and dated

Glasgow Museums and Art Galleries 2388

After 1887 Henry started
painting more frequently with
Hornel in both Glasgow and
Galloway. Female
personifications of nature now
began to appear in their work.
In the present canvas the figure
of Autumn, which blends into
the landscape, may be either a
decorative portrait or a symbol
of the season's fecundity. The
patterns of sunlight and shade
are the picture's most distinctive
characteristic. The palette,
ranging from vermilion to
orange, green and turquoise
alongside neutral tones, betrays
the influence of Monticelli,
whose paintings were displayed
at the 1886 Edinburgh
International Exhibition.

Collections
William McInnes; bequeathed by Mr
McInnes in 1944

Exhibitions
1890   GIFA (709)
1891   Royal Scottish Academy (65)
1944   *The Glasgow School,* Glasgow
        Museums and Art Galleries and
        National Gallery of Scotland,
        Edinburgh (34)
1945   *The McInnes Collection,*
        Glasgow Museums and Art
        Galleries (62)
1952   *The Early Years of the New
        English Art Club,* Birmingham
        City Art Gallery (27)
1952   *Three Centuries of Scottish
        Painting,* National Gallery of
        Canada and tour
1973   *Scottish Painting 1880-1930,*
        Glasgow Museums and Art
        Galleries (15)
1974   *Schottische Malerei,* Kunsthaus,
        Hamburg (15)
1979   *Post-Impressionism: Cross-
        currents in European Painting,*
        Royal Academy, London (306:
        illus. p. 196)

Literature
David Martin, *The Glasgow School of
Painting,* London 1897, p. 26.
James Caw, *Scottish Painting Past and
Present 1620-1908,* London 1908, p. 401.
George Buchanan, 'A Galloway
Landscape', *The Scottish Art Review 7*
(1960), p. 13.
John House and Mary-Ann Stevens
(eds.), *Post-Impressionism: Cross-currents
in European Painting,* London 1979, pp.
195 - 196.
Duncan Macmillan, *Scottish Art 1460-
1990,* Edinburgh 1990 (illus. pl. 232).
William Hardie, *Scottish Painting 1837 to
the Present,* London 1990, p. 97.

27

George Henry

A Galloway Landscape
1889
oil on canvas
121.9 x 152.4 cm
signed

Glasgow Museums and Art Galleries 2208

Henry and Hornel were as deeply influenced by the local landscape, culture and folklore as Gauguin, Bernard and Sérusier were in Brittany. Though there is no evidence that Henry accompanied Guthrie, Walton and Crawhall to Paris in 1889 or was aware of current developments, this painting, with its almost naïve, flattened landscape and colour patterns, ranks as an important Scottish contribution to European Symbolism.

Collections
Sir Thomas Dunlop, Bt.; presented by his trustees to Glasgow Museums and Art Galleries in 1940

Exhibitions
1890 GIFA (767)
1890 Glaspalast, Munich (215)
1890 Royal Scottish Academy (309)
1935 *A Century of Art in Glasgow,* Glasgow Museums and Art Galleries (147)
1938 *Empire Exhibition,* Palace of Arts, Glasgow (541)
1944 *The Glasgow School,* Glasgow Museums and Art Galleries and National Gallery of Scotland, Edinburgh (32)
1949 Royal Scottish Academy (245)
1961 *Scottish Painting,* Glasgow Museums and Art Galleries (72)
1968 *Glasgow Boys* (54)
1970 *Colour in Scottish Painting,* Glasgow Museums and Art Galleries (36)
1970 *The Glasgow School of Painting,* The Fine Art Society, London (13)
1973 *Scottish Painting 1880-1930,* Glasgow Museums and Art Galleries (16: illus.)
1974 *Schottische Malerei 1880-1930,* Kunsthaus, Hamburg (16: illus.)
1976 *150th Anniversary Exhibition,* Royal Scottish Academy Edinburgh (19)
1978 *The Discovery of Scotland,* National Gallery of Scotland (11.22)
1979 *Glasgow 1900,* The Fine Art Society, Glasgow
1990 *Scotland Creates: 5000 Years of Art and Design,* Glasgow Museums and Art Galleries (C48)

Literature
David Martin, *The Glasgow School of Painters,* London 1897, p. 26.
James Caw, *Scottish Painting Past and Present 1620-1908,* London 1908, p. 40.
Gerard Baldwin Brown, *The Glasgow School of Painters,* London 1908, pp. 7, 9, 31, 32 (illus. pl. 16).
T.J. Honeyman, *The Proceedings of the Royal Philosophical Society of Glasgow,* vol. 65, Glasgow 1941.
T.J. Honeyman, 'Art in Scotland', *The Studio* 126 (1943), pp. 67 - 68 (illus. p. 75).
George Buchanan, 'A Galloway Landscape', *The Scottish Art Review* 7 (1960), no. 4, pp. 13 - 17 (illus.).
David and Francina Irwin, *Scottish Painters at Home and Abroad 1700-1900,* London 1975, pp. 386, 392 (illus. pl. 199).
William Hardie, *Scottish Painting 1837-1939,* London 1976, pp. 80, 83 (illus. p. 176).
William Buchanan, 'Japanese Influences on the Glasgow Boys and Charles Rennie Mackintosh', *Japonisme in Art: An International Symposium,* Committee for the year 2001, Tokyo 1980.
M. Jacobs and M. Warner, *The Phaidon Guide to Art and Artists in the British Isles,* Oxford 1980 .
Worley, *British Impressionism - A Garden of Bright Images,* 1988 (illus. p. 107).
William Hardie, *Scottish Painting to the Present,* London 1990 (illus. pl. 60).
Roger Billcliffe, 'How many Swallows make a Summer? Art and Design in Glasgow in 1900', *Scotland Creates: 5000 Years of Art and Design,* London 1990, p. 140 (illus. p. 142, pl. 9.8).
Billcliffe, *The Glasgow Boys,* pp. 238, 239-240, 241-45 (illus. p. 223, pl. 215).
Duncan Macmillan, *Scottish Art 1460-1990,* Edinburgh 1990, pp. 278 - 280, 285 (illus. pl. 230).

28
George Henry

Japanese Lady with a Fan
1894
oil on canvas
61 x 40.6 cm
signed, dated and inscribed *Tokio*

Glasgow Museums and Art Galleries 1704

Many of the paintings Henry
executed during his visit to Japan
with Hornel in 1893-94 were
damaged beyond repair on the
journey home. Those that survive
show Henry's blend of bravura
technique and high-key contrasts
of brilliant and neutral colours.

Collections
Colonel Barclay Shaw; Mrs Lindesay;
presented by her to Glasgow Museums
and Art Galleries in 1927

Exhibitions
1929   *Jubilee Exhibition 1879-1929,*
        York (126)
1961   *Scottish Painting,* Glasgow
        Museums and Art Galleries (90)
1967   *Decade 1890-1900,* ACGB,
        London and tour (70)
1972   *Weltkulturen und Moderne
        Kunst,* Munich (642)
1973   *Scottish Painting 1880-1930,*
        Glasgow Museums and Art
        Galleries (17: illus.)
1974   *Schottische Malerei 1880-1930,*
        Kunsthaus, Hamburg (17: illus.)
1977   *La Peinture Britannique de
        Gainsborough à Bacon,* Musée
        des Beaux-Arts, Bordeaux (112:
        illus.)
1978-79 *Mr Henry and Mr Hornel visit
        Japan,* SAC, Glasgow Museums
        and Art Galleries and tour (60)
1991   *Art for Industry: The Glasgow-
        Japan Exchange of 1878,*
        Glasgow Museums and Art
        Galleries
1991-92 *Japan and Britain - An Aesthetic
        Dialogue 1850-1930,* Barbican
        Centre, London and tour

Literature
George Buchanan, *The Scottish Arts
Review* 7 (1960), no. 4, p. 17 (illus. p. 15).
David and Francina Irwin, *Scottish
Painters at Home and Abroad 1700-1900,*
London 1975, p. 388 (illus. p. 202).
William Buchanan, 'Henry and Hornel',

Art and Artists vol. 14, no. 1, issue 157,
pp. 12 - 17, (illus. p.15).
William Buchanan, 'Japanese Influences
on the Glasgow Boys and Charles Rennie
Mackintosh', *Japonisme in Art, An
International Symposium,* Committee for
the year 2001, Tokyo 1980.

Billcliffe, *The Glasgow Boys,* pp. 262 -
264 (illus. p. 262, pl. 243).
Antonia Lovelace, *Art for Industry, The
Glasgow Japan Exchange of 1878,*
Glasgow Museums and Art Galleries,
1991, p. 39 (illus. p. 38).

29
George Henry and Edward Atkinson Hornel

The Druids: Bringing in the Mistletoe
1890
oil on canvas
152.4 x 152.4 cm
signed jointly and dated

Glasgow Museums and Art Galleries 1534

Collections
Robert Strathern; Alexander Reid; bought from Reid by Glasgow Museums in 1922

Exhibitions
1890   Grosvenor Gallery, London (173)
1922   Walker Art Gallery, Liverpool
1924   *Canadian National Exhibition,* Toronto
1925   *British Masters Exhibition,* Bradford Art Gallery
1934   5th Annual Show, Paisley Art Institute, Paisley
1968   *Glasgow Boys* (60)
1970   *The Glasgow School of Painting,* The Fine Art Society, London (19)
1973   *Scottish Painting 1880-1930,* Glasgow Museums and Art Galleries (18: illus.)
1974   *Schottische Malerei 1880-1930,* Kunsthaus, Hamburg (18: illus.)
1990   *Scotland Creates: 5000 Years of Art and Design,* Glasgow Museums and Art Galleries (C49)

Literature
James Caw, *Scottish Painting Past and Present 1620-1908,* London 1908, p. 400.
David and Francina Irwin, *Scottish Painters at Home and Abroad 1700-1900,* London 1975, pp. 386, 389 (illus. pl. 203).
William Hardie, *Scottish Painting 1837-1939,* London 1976, pp. 80 - 81 (pl. 67).
William Buchanan, 'Japanese Influences on the Glasgow Boys and Charles Rennie Mackintosh', *Japonisme in Art, An International Symposium,* Committee for the Year 2001, Tokyo 1980.
William Buchanan (ed.), *Mackintosh's Masterwork: The Glasgow School of Art,* Glasgow 1989, p. 151 (illus.).
Billcliffe, *The Glasgow Boys,* pp. 233 - 241 (illus. p. 232, pl. 219).
William Hardie, *Scottish Painting 1837 to the Present,* London 1990, p. 98.
Duncan Macmillan, *Scottish Art 1460-1990,* Edinburgh 1990 (illus. pl. 232).

With its mixed media, rich texture and dimensional ambiguity, this masterpiece of the Glasgow School and of British *fin-de-siècle* painting bridges the gap between easel painting and decorative art. Its theme - a seasonal procession of Druids - was based directly on local tradition: the cup and ring markings in the countryside of Galloway were thought to have been made by such Celtic religious groups. The artists' use of form, colour and pattern is characteristically Symbolist, but their placement of half-length figures in the foreground anticipates northern Expressionism. The frame, designed by Henry and Hornel themselves and crowned with a lunula (or half-moon), forms an essential part of the work. A companion piece, *The Star in the East* (Glasgow Museums and Art Galleries 3137), was executed the following year.

30
Edward Atkinson Hornel

The Fish Pool
1894
oil on canvas
45.1 x 35.6 cm
signed and dated

Glasgow Museums and Art Galleries 2906

Under the influence of Matthijs
Maris in particular, Hornel often
painted groups of figures in
garden settings, both in Scotland
and, as in this case, in Japan.
Hornel's colours and technique
recall Monticelli, whose
paintings, like those of Maris,
were handled by Alexander Reid.
First shown in Scotland at the
1886 Edinburgh International
Exhibition, Monticelli's work
was prized by collectors and,
among the Glasgow Boys,
admired by Henry and Hornel.

Exhibitions
1895   Société des Beaux Arts, Glasgow
1961   *Scottish Painting,* Glasgow
        Museums and Art Galleries (94)
1967   *Decade 1890-1900,* ACGB,
        London and tour (71)
1968-69 *Three Centuries of Scottish
        Painting,* National Gallery of
        Canada, Ottawa and tour (42)
1973   *Scottish Painting 1880-1930,*
        Glasgow Museums and Art
        Galleries (21)
1974   *Schottische Malerei 1880-1930,*
        Kunsthaus, Hamburg (21)
1978-79 *Mr Henry and Mr Hornel visit
        Japan,* SAC, Glasgow Museums
        and Art Galleries and tour (71:
        illus. p. 46)
1982   *Edward Atkinson Hornel 1864-
        1933,* The Fine Art Society,
        Glasgow, Edinburgh, London
        (18)
1991   *Japan and Britain - An Aesthetic
        Dialogue 1850-1930,* Barbican
        Centre, London and tour

Literature
The Scottish Art Review 7 (1960) no. 4,
(illus. p. 17).
William R. Hardie, 'E.A. Hornel
Reconsidered', *The Scottish Art Review*
11 (1968), no. 3, p. 28, pl. 21.
David and Francina Irwin, *Scottish
Painters at Home and Abroad 1700-1900,*
London 1975, p. 388.
Billcliffe, *The Glasgow Boys,* pp. 258 -
261 (illus. p. 258, pl. 237).

31
William Kennedy

French Sketchbook
c. 1881
pencil and watercolour on paper
40 pages, book size
9.2 x 15.4 cm
inscribed on inside front cover
Will Kennedy / Paris Mar. 81

Glasgow Museums and Art Galleries 68-6

Collections
Mrs G. Irene Tuck, grand-niece of the
artist; presented by her in 1968

32
William Kennedy

Homewards
c. 1891
oil on canvas
89.3 x 141.6 cm
signed

Glasgow Museums and Art Galleries 3124

After moving south to Berkshire in the early 1890s Kennedy developed an interest in rural subjects. The scenes he painted became more idyllic, almost sentimental. The theme of the present picture - a girl leading a cow and its calf home - recalls the Hague School and especially the work of Anton Mauve, whose *Girl Leading a Cow* had been shown at the 1886 International Exhibition in Edinburgh. Kennedy's treatment of the subject is primarily atmospheric, however, and glosses over the harsher side of country life. His technique is broad; by blending the paint smoothly he creates a powdery effect. The patterning of the paint's surface owes much to Lavery.

Collections
John F. Shirreffs

Exhibitions
1892   GIFA (105)
1897   Walker Art Gallery, Liverpool
1894   Grafton Gallery, London
1961   *Scottish Painting,* Glasgow
        Museums and Art Galleries (76)
1968   *Glasgow Boys* (71)
1970   *The Glasgow School of
        Painting,* The Fine Art Society,
        London (21)
1973   *Scottish Painting 1880-1930,*
        Glasgow Museums and Art
        Galleries (25)
1974   *Schottische Malerei 1880-1930,*
        Kunsthaus, Hamburg (25)

Literature
David Martin, *The Glasgow School of Painting,* London 1897, p. 36 (illus.).
William Hardie, *Scottish Painting 1837-1939,* London 1976, p. 78.
William Hardie, *Scottish Painting 1837 to the Present,* London 1990, p. 93.

33
William Kennedy

The Fur Boa
c. 1890-93
oil on canvas
53.3 x 28.6 cm
signed

Glasgow Museums and Art Galleries 2446

At Grez in 1884 Kennedy had
been influenced by Bastien-
Lepage, with whom he had
studied in Paris. In *The Fur Boa*,
however, his debt to Whistler is
much more evident in both the
subtlety of tones and the
approach to the sitter.

Exhibitions
1944   *The Glasgow School*, Glasgow
        Museums and Art Galleries and
        the National Gallery of
        Scotland, Edinburgh
1951   *100 Years of Painting in Paisley*,
        Paisley Museum and Art
        Gallery
1968   *Glasgow Boys* (70)
1973   *Scottish Painting 1880-1930*,
        Glasgow Museums and Art
        Galleries (26: illus.)
1974   *Schottische Malerei 1880-1930*,
        Kunsthaus, Hamburg (26: illus.)
1980   *About Face Again*, Merchants
        Hall, Edinburgh
1991-92 *Japan and Britain - An Aesthetic
        Dialogue 1850-1930*, Barbican
        Centre, London and tour

Literature
William Hardie, *Scottish Painting 1837-
1939*, London 1976, p. 78.
Billcliffe, *The Glasgow Boys*, pp. 200-202
(illus. p. 202, pl. 193).
William Hardie, *Scottish Painting 1837 to
the Present*, London 1990, p. 93.

34
John Lavery

A Rally
1885
watercolour on paper
64 x 62 cm
signed and dated

Glasgow Museums and Art Galleries 1916

In 1885 Lavery turned his attention from rustic to middle-class life. This watercolour focuses on the figure of Miss MacBride in the foreground (also prominent in Aberdeen Art Gallery's related canvas of 1885, *The Tennis Party)*, shown playing in a tennis match on the courts in Cathcart, a village southwest of Glasgow. Lavery's experience as a photographer's assistant probably accounts for his interest in depicting physical action: as Billcliffe notes in *The Glasgow Boys*, the artist had already used the camera as a compositional aid as a young man.

Collections
Presented to Glasgow Museums and Art Galleries by the artist in 1935

Exhibitions
1935   *A Century of Art in Glasgow*, Glasgow Museums and Art Galleries (116)
1944   *The Glasgow School*, CEMA, Glasgow Museums and Art Galleries (25)
1951   *Loan Exhibition of Paintings by Sir John Lavery*, Belfast City Art Gallery (33)
1951   *100 Years of Painting in Paisley*, Paisley Museum and Art Gallery
1952   Birmingham City Art Gallery
1961   *Scottish Painting*, Glasgow Museums and Art Galleries (132)
1963-64   *English Watercolours of the Eighteenth to Twentieth Centuries*, Peking and Nationalgalerie, Berlin (122: illus.)

1968   *Glasgow Boys* (74)
1971   *Whistler and His World*, Wildenstein Gallery, New York and Museum of Art, Philadelphia (87)
1973   *Scottish Painting 1880-1930*, Glasgow Museums and Art Galleries (28)
1974   *Schottische Malerei 1880-1930*, Kunsthaus, Hamburg (28)
1981-82   *Sir James Guthrie and the Scottish Realists*, The Fine Art Society, Glasgow and London (67)
1983   *John Lavery, the Early Career 1880-1895*, Crawford Centre for the Arts, St Andrews and Glasgow Museums and Art Galleries (8)

Literature
Walter Shaw-Sparrow, *John Lavery and His Work*, London 1912, p. 175.
Sir John Lavery, *The Life of a Painter*, London 1940, p. 254.
The Scottish Art Review (1946) no.1, illus. p. 27.
Kenneth McConkey (introd.), *Sir John Lavery RA 1856-1941*, London 1984, pp. 29 - 30.

35
John Lavery

The 1888 Glasgow International Exhibition
1888
oil on canvas
61 x 45.7 cm
signed and dated

Glasgow Museums and Art Galleries 2504

In the summer of 1888 Lavery produced a series of works that signalled his abandonment of Bastien-Lepage's Naturalism in favour of a more decorative approach to both paint and composition. Of these works, the many sketches he made of the 1888 Glasgow International Exhibition, which won acclaim when they were exhibited at Craibe Angus's gallery in October of that year, are perhaps the most important for the breadth of their technique. This view of the Exhibition shows the approach to the large main building, designed by James Sellars, at dusk. The interior of the central dome had been decorated with allegorical figures by four of the Glasgow Boys, including Lavery himself.

Collections
Messrs Pearson and Westergaard; purchased from them in 1945.

Exhibitions
1973   *Scottish Painting 1880-1930,* Glasgow Museums and Art Galleries (29: illus.)
1974   *Schottische Malerei 1880-1930,* Kunsthaus, Hamburg (29: illus.)
1979   *Glasgow 1900,* The Fine Art Society, Glasgow
1983   *John Lavery - The Early Career 1880-1895,* Crawford Centre for the Arts, St Andrews and Glasgow Museums and Art Galleries (28)
1990   Glasgow

Literature
Billcliffe, *The Glasgow Boys,* pp. 216 - 224 (illus. p. 224, pl. 216).
Burkhauser, *Glasgow Girls* (illus. p. 27, pl. 15).

36
Frances Macdonald

Autumn
1898
pencil and watercolour on vellum
45.4 x 14.9 cm
signed and dated

Glasgow Museums and Art Galleries
77-13a

The beaten lead frame was
designed and worked by the
artist specifically for this
watercolour. See also cat. 38.

For a biographical note on Frances
Macdonald, see page 119.

Collections
Talwin Morris; Mrs Alice Talwin Morris;
presented by her to Glasgow Museums in
1939

Exhibitions
1978-79 *Mackintosh Watercolours,*
        Glasgow Museums and Art
        Galleries and tour (6)
1990   Glasgow (159)

Literature
Billcliffe, *Mackintosh Watercolours,* p.46
(illus. p. 67).
Roger Billcliffe, 'How many Swallows
make a Summer? Art and Design in
Glasgow in 1900', *Scotland Creates: 5000
Years of Art and Design,* London 1990, p.
144 (illus. 9, 11).

See also cat. 81, 82 and 97.

37
Margaret Macdonald

Summer
c. 1893
pencil, pen and ink and
watercolour on paper
51.7 x 21.8 cm

*The Hunterian Art Gallery (Mackintosh
Collection), University of Glasgow
Sb)1*

This watercolour may be the
*Design for a Window of Mosaic
Glass* with which Margaret
Macdonald won a prize in the
Glasgow School of Art Local
Design Competition of 1894. Be
that as it may, it is an important
example of the 'Spook School'
style of the early 1890s and
contrasts starkly with the more
illustrative drawings of the late
1890s. The female figure is
closely related to Frances
Macdonald's *Morning*, a beaten
brass wall sconce of
approximately 1896 (Glasgow
Museums and Art Galleries
46.5b).

For a biographical note on Margaret
Macdonald, see page 119.

Collections
Mackintosh Estate; University of
Glasgow

Exhibitions
1899   International Society for
        Sculptors, Painters and Gravers,
        London (209)
1933   *Mackintosh Memorial
        Exhibition* (165, as by C.R.
        Mackintosh)
1968   *Charles Rennie Mackintosh*,
        Edinburgh and tour (62)
1971   *Burne-Jones*, Sheffield Art
        Galleries (227)
1973   *Glasgow University's Pictures*,
        P. & D. Colnaghi, London (63)
1976-77 *Women Artists*, Los Angeles
        County Museum of Art and
        tour
1978   Glasgow (i)
1983   *Margaret Macdonald
        Mackintosh 1864-1933*,
        Hunterian Art Gallery, Glasgow
1990   Glasgow
1992   *Charles Rennie Mackintosh
        Drawings, Designs and
        Watercolours*, Hunterian Art
        Gallery, Glasgow

Literature
The Magazine, April 1897.
Billcliffe, *Mackintosh Watercolours*, p. 46
(illus. p. 62).
Michael Donnelly, *Glasgow Stained
Glass*, Glasgow 1985 (illus. p. 31).
Pamela Reekie, *Margaret Macdonald
Mackintosh*, 1983 (illus. 3).
Jean-Claude Garcias, *Mackintosh*, Paris
1989 (illus. p. 25).
William Hardie, *Scottish Painting 1837-
1939*, London 1976, p. 84.
Burkhauser, *Glasgow Girls*, p. 110 (illus.
fig. 138).
Pamela Robertson, *Charles Rennie
Mackintosh at the Hunterian*, 1991, p. 16
(illus. p. 17).

38
Margaret Macdonald

Winter
1898
pencil and watercolour on vellum
47.2 x 19.6 cm
signed and dated

Glasgow Museums and Art Galleries
77-13b

In the 1890s Margaret and
Frances Macdonald devoted at
least two series of watercolours
to the seasons. The earlier, highly
Symbolist watercolours they
produced during the first half of
the decade are important
examples of the Celtic 'Spook
School' work of The Four.
Generally, the later watercolours
are more illustrative than
interpretative, and reject the
figural gauntness of the earlier
ones. The Macdonalds designed
and executed the lead frames for
both series in their workshop at
128 Hope Street toward the end
of the period. Each frame is
decorated with symbols of each
season. See also cat. 36.

Collections
Talwin Morris; Mrs Alice Talwin Morris;
presented by her to Glasgow Museums in
1939

Exhibitions
1933   *Mackintosh Memorial*
        Exhibition, McLellan Galleries,
        Glasgow
1978-79 *Mackintosh Watercolours*,
        Glasgow Museums and Art
        Galleries and tour (7)
1990   Glasgow (161)

Literature
Billcliffe, *Mackintosh Watercolours*, p. 46
(illus. p. 67).
Roger Billcliffe, 'How many Swallows
make a Summer? Art and Design in
Glasgow in 1900', *Scotland Creates: 5000
Years of Art and Design*, London 1990,
p. 144 (illus. 9. 11a).

See also cat. 96 and 97.

39
James Pittendrigh Macgillivray

The Tea Table
1885
oil on canvas
38.2 x 46.3 cm
signed with initials and dated

Edinburgh City Museums and Art
Galleries 202.1964

Macgillivray was the only
sculptor associated with the
Glasgow School. His paintings
are rare and, like his sculpture,
possess qualities more formal and
academic than innovative.

Collections
Robert Macaulay Stevenson; the Scottish
Modern Arts Association; presented to
the City of Edinburgh in 1964

Exhibitions
1944   *The Glasgow School,* Glasgow
        Museums and Art Galleries (84)
1944   Royal Scottish Society of
        Painters in Watercolours, Royal

Scottish Academy, Edinburgh
(46)
1968   *Glasgow Boys* (80)

40
William York Macgregor

Leafy Lane
1898
lithograph on paper
16 x 19 cm
signed and dated proof copy

Glasgow Museums and Art Galleries
U-261a

Charles Rennie Mackintosh

Part Seen, Imagined Part
1896
pencil and watercolour on tracing paper
39.0 x 19.5 cm
signed and dated April 1896 and inscribed *Part/Seen/Imag/Ined/Part*

Glasgow Museums and Art Galleries 77.13aq

This design, a hybrid of figure and tree forms, evinces Mackintosh's commitment to symbolism in the mid-1890s. The figure was reworked as a full-size stencil repeat motif in the artist's design for the wall decoration of the Ladies' Tea Room in Miss Cranston's Buchanan Street Tea Rooms (see fig. 3.4, p. 105). The paper is severely discoloured. The frame was probably designed by Talwin Morris.

Collections
Talwin Morris; Mrs Alice Talwin Morris; presented by her to Glasgow Museums in 1939

Exhibitions
1896   Arts and Crafts Exhibition Society, London (589)
1933   *Mackintosh Memorial Exhibition*, McLellan Galleries, Glasgow (82)
1975   *British Painting 1900-1960*, Sheffield City Gallery
1978-79 *Mackintosh Watercolours*, Glasgow Museums and Art Galleries and tour (51)
1983   *Victorian Prints and Watercolours*, Glasgow Museums and Art Galleries

Literature
Billcliffe, *Mackintosh Watercolours*, p. 30 (illus. p. 71).
Thomas Howarth, *Charles Rennie Mackintosh and the Modern Movement*, London 1990, p. 38.
Burkhauser, *Glasgow Girls* (illus. p. 118, fig. 149).
Julian Halsby, *Scottish Watercolours 1740-1940*, London 1986, p. 175.

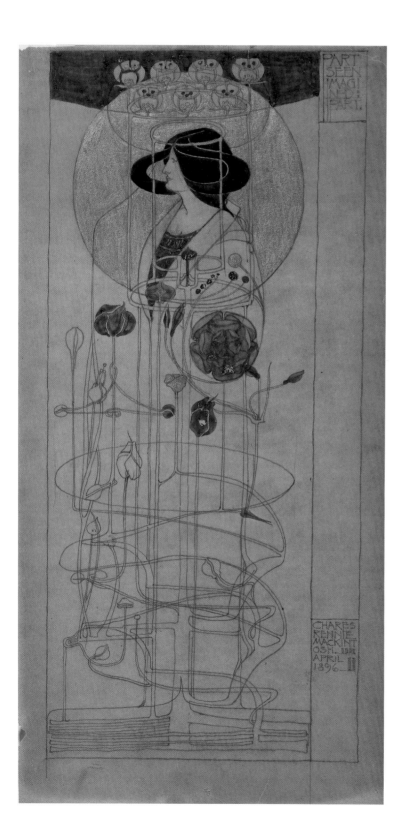

42

Charles Rennie Mackintosh

Pinks
c. 1922-23
watercolour on paper
50.1 x 50.1 cm
signed

Glasgow Museums and Art Galleries 2247

At Walberswick, Suffolk, in 1914 and 1915, Mackintosh had produced a series of highly finished flower studies in which the natural forms of the plants were overlaid with a sense of pattern. He further intensified this rationalisation in a number of semi-abstract watercolours of cut flowers, which he painted in Chelsea around 1916-20. However, in their synthesis of formal and organic patterns and in their mix of broad washes and detailed areas of strong colour, the artist's still lifes of circa 1922-24 anticipate the French landscapes he executed between 1923 and 1927.

The colours of the exhibited watercolour have faded.

Collections
John Sawyers; presented by him to Glasgow Museums in 1941

Exhibitions
1933   *Mackintosh Memorial Exhibition,* McLellan Galleries, Glasgow (159: purchased John Sawyers)
1953   *Charles Rennie Mackintosh,* Saltire Society and ACGB, Edinburgh (A.1)
1963-64 *English Watercolours of the Eighteenth to the Twentieth Centuries,* Peking and Nationalgalerie, Berlin (132)
1968   *Charles Rennie Mackintosh,* Royal Scottish Museum, Edinburgh and tour (330)
1970   *Colour in Scottish Painting,* Glasgow Museums and Art Galleries (52)
1973   *Scottish Painting 1880-1930,* Glasgow Museums and Art Galleries (33: illus.)
1974   *Schottische Malerei 1880-1930,* Kunsthaus, Hamburg (33: illus.)
1977   *Flower Drawings by Charles Rennie Mackintosh,* Hunterian Museum, Glasgow (40)
1978-79 *Mackintosh Watercolours,* Glasgow Museums and Art Galleries and tour (175)
1980   *Royal Scottish Society of Painters in Watercolours Centenary*

Exhibition, Royal Scottish Academy, Edinburgh (77)
1982   *Flower Drawings by Charles Rennie Mackintosh,* The Aldeburgh Festival Sociey, Aldeburgh, Suffolk

Literature
The Studio 86 (1923), p. 381.
The Scottish Art Review 9 (1974), no. 4 (illus. p. 27).
Billcliffe, *Mackintosh Watercolours,* p. 41 (illus. p. 109).
Julian Halsby, *Scottish Watercolours 1740-1940,* London 1986, p. 203.

43
Charles Rennie Mackintosh

The Grey Iris
c. 1922-24
watercolour on paper
43.1 x 37.4 cm
signed

Glasgow Museums and Art Galleries 1855

Exhibitions
1925   *Fifth International Exhibition of Watercolour Paintings,* Chicago
1933   *Mackintosh Memorial Exhibition,* McLellan Galleries, Glasgow (70: purchased Glasgow Museums)
1953   *Charles Rennie Mackintosh,* The Saltire Society and ACGB, Edinburgh (A.12)
1973   *Scottish Painting 1880-1930,* Glasgow Museums and Art Galleries (32)
1974   *Schottische Malerei 1880-1930,* Kunsthaus, Hamburg (32)
1977   *Flower Drawings by Charles Rennie Mackintosh,* Hunterian Museum, Glasgow
1978-79 *Mackintosh Watercolours,* Glasgow Museums and Art Galleries and tour (174)
1985-86 *Charles Rennie Mackintosh,* Tokyo and Japanese tour (14)

Literature
Billcliffe, *Mackintosh Watercolours,* p. 41 (illus. p. 103)

44
Charles Rennie Mackintosh

Port Vendres, La Ville
c. 1924-26
watercolour on paper
44.4 x 44.7 cm
signed

Glasgow Museums and Art Galleries 1856

Perhaps on the advice of John
Duncan Fergusson, a Francophile
Scottish painter whom they had
known in London, the
Mackintoshes lived in the south
of France in 1923-27. Initially
they settled in Collioure but then
moved to Port Vendres near the
Franco-Spanish border. During
the summer months the
Mackintoshes moved higher into
the mountains to Mont Luis,
within easy reach of La Lagonne
(cat. 45).
Mackintosh had already started
painting landscapes in 1920,
during a visit to Dorset. In his
French watercolours he searched
for structure and pattern in the
landscape, which is sometimes
startlingly clear.

Exhibitions
1933   *Mackintosh Memorial
      Exhibition,* McLellan Galleries,
      Glasgow (188a)
1938   *Empire Exhibition,* Palace of
      Arts, Glasgow (222)
1953   *Charles Rennie Mackintosh,*
      The Saltire Society and ACGB,
      Edinburgh (A.4)
1954   *Royal Scottish Society of Painters
      in Watercolour Centenary
      Exhibition,* Royal Scottish
      Academy, Edinburgh (78)
1961   *Scottish Painting,* Glasgow
      Museums and Art Galleries
      (138)
1978-79 *Mackintosh Watercolours,*
      Glasgow Museums and Art
      Galleries and tour (186)
1985-86 *Charles Rennie Mackintosh,*
      Tokyo and Japanese tour (15)

Literature
Artwork 6, no. 21, p. 28.
The Studio 105 (1933), p. 345.
Billcliffe, *Mackintosh Watercolours,* p. 42
(illus. p. 123).

45
Charles Rennie Mackintosh

The Village of La Lagonne
c. 1924-27
watercolour on paper
45.7 x 45.7 cm
signed

Glasgow Museums and Art Galleries
60-24

Collections
Purchased at Mackintosh Memorial
Exhibition (1933) by T.M. Whyte; with J.
& R. Edmiston, Glasgow, 1960

Exhibitions
1933 *Mackintosh Memorial*
       Exhibition, McLellan Galleries,
       Glasgow (58)
1961 *Scottish Painting*, Glasgow
       Museums and Art Galleries
       (140)
1968 *Charles Rennie Mackintosh*,
       Royal Scottish Museum,
       Edinburgh and tour (342)
1973 *Scottish Painting 1880-1930*,
       Glasgow Museums and Art
       Galleries (34)
1974 *Schottische Malerei 1880-1930*,
       Kunsthaus, Hamburg (34)
1975 *British Painting 1900-1960*, City
       Art Gallery, Sheffield (99)
1978-79 *Mackintosh Watercolours*,
       Glasgow Museums and Art
       Galleries and tour (188)
1985-86 *Charles Rennie Mackintosh*,
       Tokyo and Japanese tour (17)

Literature
Billcliffe, *Mackintosh Watercolours*, p. 43
(illus. p. 130).
Charles Rennie Mackintosh, Tokyo 1985
(illus. p. 49).
Julian Halsby, *Scottish Watercolours
1740-1940*, London 1986, p. 205 (illus.
pl. 7).

See also cat. 83-95.

46
Bessie MacNicol

A Girl of the 'Sixties'
1899
oil on canvas
81.3 x 60.9 cm
signed and dated

Glasgow Museums and Art Galleries 2493

In the late 1890s Bessie MacNicol
painted a series of oils of young
women which she called her
'fancy portraits'. These were
usually self-portraits wearing
fancy dress. Guthrie and Gauld
had already painted women
seated or standing in dappled
sunlight under trees. MacNicol's
canvas unifies the figure and the
landscape. Its sensual
combination of pattern, colour
and form recalls the work of her
friend Hornel, whose example
had recently inspired her to
lighten her palette.

Collections
John Keppie; bequeathed by him in 1945

Exhibitions
1979   Scottish Society of Women
        Artists, Royal Scottish
        Academy, Edinburgh
1988   *Glasgow Girls: Women at the
        Art School 1880-1920*, Glasgow
        School of Art
1990   Glasgow (181)

Literature
Burkhauser, *Glasgow Girls*, p. 195 (illus.
p. 196, fig. 266).

Arthur Melville

A Bazaar in Cairo
c. 1881
watercolour on paper
51.2 x 36.7 cm
signed

Glasgow Museums and Art Galleries 2438

Melville had begun to explore the transparent qualities of watercolour at Grez in 1879. By the following year he was using broad washes of thin colour which allowed substantial amounts of white paper to show through. In his search for new colour experience, Melville travelled to the Middle East in the autumn of 1880, visiting Istanbul, Cairo, Baghdad and Karachi. The brilliant sunlight and intense heat, as well as the landscapes and cultures so different from his own, all had a lasting impact. His palette lightened, and the muted tones of the late 1870s inspired by Corot and Bastien-Lepage gave way to astonishingly bold colour combinations. *A Bazaar in Cairo* gives a vivid impression of sun and shadow as it records bustling city life.

Collections
William McInnes; bequeathed by him in 1944

Exhibitions
1883   Royal Scottish Academy, Edinburgh (937)
1883   Royal Institute of Painters in Watercolours (695)
1945   *The McInnes Collection,* Glasgow Museums and Art Galleries (57)

Literature
Agnes E. McKay, *Arthur Melville,* London 1951, pp. 62, 129 (illus. pl. 14).

48
Arthur Melville

Kirkwall
1886
watercolour on paper
36 x 55 cm
signed, dated and inscribed with
title

Glasgow Museums and Art Galleries 65.5

In 1885 and 1886 Melville and Guthrie together visited the Orkney Islands, which lie north of the Scottish mainland. Though Melville often worked his watercolours up in the studio, by this time they had become highly atmospheric. This particular work depicts the fifteenth-century cathedral of St Magnus and, in the foreground, field gleaners at work, but is primarily an evocation of the cool autumnal climate of Orkney, with its grey, oppressive skies.

Exhibitions
1977-78 *Arthur Melville 1855-1904,*
　　　　Dundee Museums and Art
　　　　Galleries and tour (16)
1983　　*Victorian Prints and*
　　　　Watercolours, Glasgow
　　　　Museums and Art Galleries

Literature
Billcliffe, *The Glasgow Boys,* p. 193 (illus. pl. 183).
Duncan Macmillan, *Scottish Art 1460-1990,* Edinburgh 1990, p. 286 (illus. pl. 236).

49
Arthur Melville

A Mediterranean Port
1892
watercolour on paper
51.3 x 78.2 cm
signed and dated

Glasgow Museums and Art Galleries 1702

Executed during a visit to Spain in 1892, *A Mediterranean Port* marked a return to the dazzling light effects of Melville's earlier Middle Eastern tour. Using strong colours and a 'blottesque' technique, Melville moved towards greater luminosity and simplication of form. Theodore Roussel, a close friend, described Melville's method of working on wet paper and applying the watercolour in pools:
Melville's method was pure watercolour, but watercolour applied on a specially prepared paper. This paper was soaked in dilute Chinese white, till it was literally saturated and impregnated with white. He worked often into a wet surface, sponging out superfluous detail, running in those warm browns and rich blues and reds which he knew so well how to blend and simplify. His colour was often dropped on the paper in rich, full spots or blobs rather than applied with any definite brushmarks. The colour floats into little pools, with the white of the ground softening each touch [....] those blobs in his drawings, which seem so meaningless, disordered and chaotic, are actually organised with the utmost care to lead the way to the foreseen result.
Quoted by R. Fedden, 'Arthur Melville RWS', *Proceedings of the Old Watercolour Society*, 1923-24, p. 41.

Collections
Col. Barclay Shaw; Mrs M.D. Lindsay; presented by her to Glasgow Museums and Art Galleries in 1927

Exhibitions
1977-78 *Arthur Melville 1855-1904*, Dundee Museums and Art Galleries and tour (40)

Literature
William Hardie, *Scottish Painting 1837-1939*, London 1976, p. 89.
Billcliffe, *The Glasgow Boys*, p. 272 (illus. p. 271, pl. 253).

50
Arthur Melville

Autumn - Loch Lomond
1893
watercolour on paper
59 x 85 cm
signed and dated

Glasgow Museums and Art Galleries
66-15

Autumn - Loch Lomond
demonstrates Melville's
'blottesque' technique in
watercolour, used here to capture
the essential colours of the
autumnal Scottish landscape.

Exhibitions
1970   *Colour in Scottish Painting*,
        Glasgow Museums and Art
        Galleries (58)
1973   *Scottish Painting 1880-1930*,
        Glasgow Museums and Art
        Galleries (38: illus.)
1974   *Schottische Malerei 1880-1930*,
        Kunsthaus, Hamburg (38: illus.)
1977-78 *Arthur Melville 1855-1904*,
        Dundee Museums and Art
        Galleries and tour (45)
1983   *Victorian Prints and*
        Watercolours, Glasgow
        Museums and Art Galleries

Literature
Billcliffe, *The Glasgow Boys*, p. 270 (illus.
p. 278, pl. 260).
Stephen Quiller, *Colour Choices*, New
York 1989 (illus. p. 134).

51
Arthur Melville

An Eastern Harbour
1894
watercolour on paper
58.5 x 85 cm
signed and dated

Glasgow Museums and Art Galleries 2904

Collections
Mrs J.S.S. Christie-Crawfurd; bequeathed
by her in 1951

Exhibitions
1961   *Scottish Painting*, Glasgow
      Museums and Art Galleries
      (124)
1963-64 *English Watercolours of the
      Eighteenth to Twentieth
      Centuries*, Peking and
      Nationalgalerie, Berlin
1966   Links House (34)
1967   Montrose Festival
1970   *Colour in Scottish Painting*,
      Glasgow Museums and Art
      Galleries (59)

1973   *Scottish Painting 1880-1930,*
      Glasgow Museums and Art
      Galleries (39)
1974   *Schottische Malerei 1880-1930,*
      Kunsthaus, Hamburg (39)
1977-78 *Arthur Melville 1855-1904,*
      Dundee Museums and Art
      Galleries and tour (5)

52
Stuart Park

Roses
1889
oil on canvas
40.7 x 66 cm
signed in monogram and dated

Glasgow Museums and Art Galleries 2504

Collections
Messrs Pearson and Westergaard;
purchased from them in 1945

Exhibitions
1890   GIFA (737)
1961   *Scottish Painting,* Glasgow
        Museums and Art Galleries (80)
1968   *Glasgow Boys* (95)
1970   *Colour in Scottish Painting,*
        Glasgow Museums and Art
        Galleries (62)
1970   *The Glasgow School of
        Painting,* The Fine Art Society,
        London (31)
1973   *Scottish Painting 1880-1930,*
        Glasgow Museums and Art
        Galleries (41)
1974   *Schottische Malerei 1880-1930,*
        Kunsthaus, Hamburg (41)

Literature
George Buchanan, 'Scottish Art from the
Nineteenth Century', *The Scottish Field,*
October 1961, pp. 106 - 08.
William Hardie, *Scottish Painting 1837-
1939,* London 1976, p. 81 (illus. pl. 79).
Billcliffe, *The Glasgow Boys,* pp. 268 -
269 (illus. p. 268, pl. 249).
William Hardie, *Scottish Painting 1937 to
the Present,* London 1990, p. 15.

53
James Paterson

The Last Turning, Winter,
Moniaive
1885
oil on canvas
61.3 x 91.4 cm
signed, dated and inscribed
Moniaive recto and signed, dated
and inscribed with title verso

Glasgow Museums and Art Galleries 3349

Just as Guthrie settled into a rural
environment at Cockburnspath,
so Paterson immersed himself in
the life of Moniaive, a small town
in Dumfriesshire. Initially
attracted by the local scenery and
the drama of the changing
seasons of southwest Scotland, he
developed a Realist approach to
landscape painting based on
formal values. In contrast to
many of the other Glasgow Boys,
Paterson did not rely on the
compositional devices and
techniques recently developed by
Bastien-Lepage. Instead, he chose
to involve his audience by means
of his atmospheric, dramatic and
direct style and academic
compositions. The introduction
of a single figure in this canvas is
characteristic.

Collections
James Ross, Aberdeen, 1885; Mrs M.C.
Wemyss Honeyman; purchased by
Glasgow Museums at Wemyss
Honeyman sale, Christie's & Edmiston's,
Glasgow, 1979

Exhibitions
1982   *Thank You Very Much,*
        Glasgow Museums and Art
        Galleries (40)
1983   *Landscape in Britain 1850-1950,*
        ACGB, Hayward Gallery,
        London and tour (75)
1983-84 James Paterson, *Moniaive and*
        Following Family Traditions,
        Lillie Art Gallery, Milngavie,
        and tour (8)

Literature
Billcliffe, *The Glasgow Boys,* pp. 163 -
168 (illus. p. 167, pl. 162).

54
James Paterson

Morton from Keir
1893
watercolour on paper
33 x 50.2 cm
signed, dated and inscribed *Keir*

Glasgow Museums and Art Galleries 2816

Collections
Andrew Paterson; Miss M.A. Paterson,
by whom bequeathed 1948

Exhibitions
1901   Glasgow International
        Exhibition (1002: lent by
        Andrew Paterson)
1938   Empire Exhibition, Glasgow,
        (184: lent by Miss Paterson)
1983-84 James Paterson, *Moniaive and
        Continuing Family Traditions,*
        Lillie Art Gallery, Milngavie and
        tour (16)

55
John Quinton Pringle

Bob
1891
watercolour on paper
55 x 34.5 cm
signed and dated

Glasgow Museums and Art Galleries 2677

This portrait is said to represent
Robert Hood, one of the artist's
fellow part-time students at
Glasgow School of Art. Insofar
as it evinces Pringle's growing
interest in surface pattern, it
shows the influence of Guthrie's
direct, unsentimental approach to
portraiture of the mid-1880s (see
Old Willie, cat. 21). Like Guthrie,
Pringle also used lettering as a
decorative compositional device.

Collections
John W. Pringle; presented by him to
Glasgow Museums 1947

Exhibitions
1946 *Pictures by John Quinton Pringle*,
Saltire Club, Glasgow (22)
1961 *Scottish Painting*, Glasgow
Museums and Art Galleries (131)
1964 *John Q. Pringle (1864-1925), A
Centenary Exhibition*, Glasgow Museums
and Art Galleries (74)
1968 *John Quinton Pringle*, SAC,
GAGM and tour
1973 *John Quinton Pringle*, Edinburgh
City Art Centre
1981-82 *John Quinton Pringle*, SAC,
Glasgow and tour (48)

Literature
Ian McClure, 'John Quinton Pringle', *Art
and Artists*, 1981, p. 15 (illus. p. 16).

56
John Quinton Pringle

Muslin Street, Bridgeton
1895-96
oil on canvas
35.9 x 41.2 cm
signed and dated 93

Edinburgh City Museums and Art
Galleries 96.1964

The painting shows a bird's eye
view of a typical Glasgow street
in the mid-1890s. One of the
artist's favourite pictures, at the
time of its sale in 1922 he dated it
(erroneously) 1893. It cannot
predate 1895 as it represents the
view from the roof of the house
in Muslin Street to which a
younger brother, Donald Pringle,
and family had moved that
spring.

Collections
The Scottish Modern Arts Association
(purchased 1922); presented to the City
of Edinburgh 1964

Exhibitions
19??   Glasgow School of Art (25)
1938   Glasgow Empire Exhibition
        (243)
1939   *Scottish Art*, Royal Academy,
        London (361)
1944   Royal Scottish Society of
        Painters in Watercolours, Royal
        Scottish Academy, Edinburgh
        (153)
1973   *100 Jahre Schottische Kunst*,
        Bayerischen Vereinsbank,
        Munich (12)
1978   *The Discovery of Scotland*,
        National Gallery of Scotland,
        Edinburgh (12.27)
1981-82 *John Quinton Pringle*, SAC,
        Glasgow and tour

57
John Quinton Pringle

Child's Head
c. 1896-99
watercolour on ivorine
3.8 x 3 cm

Glasgow Museums and Art Galleries 2678

58
John Quinton Pringle

Woman's Head
c. 1896-99
watercolour on ivorine
7.2 x 7.3 cm

Glasgow Museums and Art Galleries 2679

59
John Quinton Pringle

Boy in Red Cap and Small Girl
c. 1896-99
watercolour on ivorine
7.8 x 6.0 cm

Glasgow Museums and Art Galleries 2680

As a professional optician and instrument-maker, Pringle was intrigued by colour in art and by miniatures. The earliest of these tiny but exquisite paintings date from the mid-1890s. Given their scale, they were particularly well suited to child portraiture. Pringle's small output included several important commissions, most notably for portraits of Fra Newbery's two daughters and William Davidson's three sons. (Mackintosh had designed Windyhill for Davidson.) The artist continued to paint miniatures until the First World War. His amateur status notwithstanding, his work was exhibited at home and abroad. In 1902 he contributed to the XV Vienna Secession, possibly at the instigation of either Newbery or Mackintosh. Pringle's work was shown in London at the Doré Gallery in 1905, and in 1914 in the Whitechapel Art Gallery's *Twentieth Century Art Exhibition.*

Collections
Donald S. Pringle; John W. Pringle; presented by him to Glasgow Museums in 1947

Possibly a study of Mrs Donald Pringle.

Collections
Donald S. Pringle; John W. Pringle; presented by him to Glasgow Museums in 1947

The children may be the artist's nephew and niece.

Collections
Donald S. Pringle; John W. Pringle; presented by him to Glasgow Museums in 1947

60

John Quinton Pringle

Two Figures and a Fence
1904
oil on canvas
25.4 x 30.5 cm
signed and dated

Glasgow Museums and Art Galleries 2662

The opening of Pringle's shop in 1896 had freed him from the necessity of selling his work but at the same time restricted the amount of time he had to paint. He experimented increasingly nevertheless, and from about 1900 his colours brightened and his brushstrokes became smaller and looser. The present canvas was executed in two stages, the landscape painted in 1903 during a visit to Port Ellen on Islay, off the west coast of Scotland, and the figures added the following year. The two parts of the painting are visually united by Pringle's fragmentary brushwork, possibly inspired by Le Sidaner, who exhibited his work regularly at the Glasgow Institute between 1903 and 1906.

Collections
John W. Pringle; presented by him to Glasgow Museums in 1947

Exhibitions
1946   Saltire Club Exhibition (14)
1964   *John Quinton Pringle (1864-1925), A Centenary Exhibition,* Glasgow Museums and Art Galleries (68)
1968   *John Quinton Pringle,* SAC, GAGM and tour
1973   *John Quinton Pringle,* City Art Centre, Edinburgh
1973   *Spring Exhibition,* Paisley Art Institute (51)
1973   *Scottish Painting 1880-1930,* Glasgow Museums and Art Galleries (48)
1974   *Schottische Malerei,* Kunsthaus, Hamburg (48)
1975-76 *British Painting 1900-1960,* Mappin Art Gallery, Sheffield

and Aberdeen Art Gallery (139)
1981-82 *John Quinton Pringle,* SAC, Glasgow and tour (24)

Literature
William Hardie, *Scottish Painting 1837-1939,* London 1976 (illus. pl. 83).

John Quinton Pringle

On the River Sainte-Gertrude,
Caudebec, Normandy
1910
oil on canvas
43 x 53.5 cm
signed and dated

Glasgow Museums and Art Galleries 3306

In 1910 Pringle spent about ten
days painting in Caudebec,
Normandy. The four known
paintings from that visit (of
which the present canvas is the
largest) were executed with a
square brush in the manner of the
Glasgow Boys. Pringle did not
use oil paints again until 1921.

Collections
D.A. Turnbull; his daughter; James
Meldrum; presented by him to Glasgow
Museums in 1973

Exhibitions
1922   J.Q. Pringle, *Glasgow School of*
        Art (30)
1925   RGIFA (282)
1964   *John Q. Pringle (1864-1925), A*
        Centenary Exhibition, Glasgow
        Museums and Art Galleries (62)
1968   *John Quinton Pringle,* SAC,
        GAGM and tour
1973   *Spring Exhibition,* Paisley Art
        Institute (50)
1973   *John Quinton Pringle,*
        Edinburgh City Art Centre
1977   *25 Glorious Years,* Glasgow
        Museums and Art Galleries (99)
1981-82 *John Quinton Pringle,* SAC,
        Glasgow and tour (28)

62
Robert Macaulay Stevenson

Moonrise
c. 1892-1900
oil on canvas
111.8 x 76.2 cm
signed

Glasgow Museums and Art Galleries 1670

In the mid-1880s Stevenson, like
Guthrie and Walton, had
explored the themes and values of
the Barbizon painters, especially
their use of local harmonies and
their subject matter. However, in
the late 1880s Naturalism gave
way to a more atmospheric style
inspired by Corot. Over the next
two decades Stevenson produced
a number of woodland
landscapes dominated by hazy
blue sunlight (or, more
frequently, moonlight) and tall
silver birches.

Collections
Charles E. Lichfield-Knox; bequeathed
by him to Glasgow Museums 1926

63
Edward Arthur Walton

A Surrey Meadow - Morning
1880
oil on canvas
76.8 x 121.9 cm
signed and dated

Glasgow Museums and Art Galleries 2485

During the summer of 1880 Walton visited southeast England. Judging from the present canvas, the artist developed many of the ideas he had had the previous year, when he abandoned his dark tonalities. His dreamy, atmospheric landscapes of the 1880s contrast sharply with those of many of the other Boys, most notably Guthrie and Lavery. The hazy sunlight and shade, wispy tree forms and grazing cattle betray Walton's indebtedness to Corot, Troyon and the Hague School with respect both to composition and detail.

Collections
W. Gilchrist Macbeth; W.R. Hall; with Doig, Wilson and Wheatley, Edinburgh 1945

Exhibitions
1881   GIFA (424)
1973   *Scottish Painting,* University Art Gallery, Halifax, Canada (as *Ayrshire Pastoral*)
1973   *Scottish Painting 1880-1930,* Glasgow Museums and Art Galleries (54: as *Ayrshire Pastoral*)
1974   *Schottische Malerei 1880-1930,* Kunsthaus, Hamburg (54: as *Ayrshire Pastoral*)

Literature
G.R. Halkett (ed.), *Notes to the Twentieth Exhibition of The Glasgow Institute of the Fine Arts,* Glasgow 1881, p. 61 (illus. by line drawing).
Billcliffe, *The Glasgow Boys,* p. 44 (illus. pl. 31).

64
Edward Arthur Walton

Rosneath
c. 1883
watercolour on paper
33.6 x 49.4 cm
signed

Glasgow Museums and Art Galleries 2497

Rosneath is one of several watercolours of rural scenes that immediately predated a series of Helensburgh townscapes in Walton's oeuvre.

Collections
John Keppie; bequeathed by him in 1945

Exhibitions
1966   Links House (19)
1967   Montrose Festival
1972   *Helensburgh and the Glasgow School*, Victoria Halls, Helensburgh (28)
1972   *Scenic Aspects of the River Clyde*, Glasgow Museums and Art Galleries (68)

Literature
Billcliffe, *The Glasgow Boys*, p. 137 (illus. pl. 127).

65
Edward Arthur Walton

Seaside Cottages with Dovecot
c. 1883
watercolour on paper
34 x 52.7 cm
signed

Glasgow Museums and Art Galleries 66-7

The present canvas was almost certainly painted at Cockburnspath, where Walton spent the summers of 1883 and 1884 with Guthrie. The red roof pantiles and the whitewashed walls are typical of vernacular house design in the area. As in Rosneath, Walton used a dry brush technique to add surface texture; this is particularly noticeable here in his painting of the stony road surface.

Exhibitions
1970   *Colour in Scottish Painting*,
        Glasgow Museums and Art
        Galleries
1986   *Academics and Revolutionaries*,
        Glasgow Museums and Art
        Galleries

66

Edward Arthur Walton

The Gamekeeper's Daughter
1886
watercolour on paper
43.5 x 34.5 cm
signed recto and inscribed, verso,
in pencil *Phyllis/No. 2*

Glasgow Museums and Art Galleries 2103

Inspired by the work of Bastien-
Lepage, the drawing
demonstrates Walton's mastery
of watercolour and his keen
interest in textural effects. The
flesh tones were crafted with
particular care, while the slightly
rough surfaces of the background
and the smock were achieved
with light strokes of a dry brush.
The watercolour was exhibited at
the RSW in 1886 under the title
Phyllis, which name is inscribed
on the reverse. Nothing else is
known about the sitter.

Collections
Miss Betty Paterson; presented by her in
1938

Exhibitions
1938   Empire Exhibition, Glasgow
        (187: lent by Miss Paterson)
1944   *The Glasgow School,* C.E.M.A.,
        Glasgow Museums and Art
        Galleries (18)
1961   *Scottish Painting,* Glasgow
        Museums and Art Galleries
        (133)
1973   *Scottish Painting 1880-1930,*
        Glasgow Museums and Art
        Galleries (55)
1974   *Schottische Malerei 1880-1930,*
        Kunsthaus, Hamburg (55)
1983   *Victorian Prints and
        Watercolours,* Glasgow
        Museums and Art Galleries
1986   *Academics and Revolutionaries,*
        Glasgow Museums and Art
        Galleries

Literature
Billcliffe, *The Glasgow Boys,* pp. 144 -
145 (illus. p. 155, pl. 145).
Duncan Macmillan, *Scottish Art 1460-
1990,* Edinburgh 1990 (illus. pl. 221).

3.9 George Walton (designer),
'Gather ye rosebuds while ye may',
detail of stained glass window by
J. & W. Guthrie for 4 Devonshire
Gardens, Glasgow, 1892. Photograph
Glasgow Museums and Art Galleries,
reproduced by kind permission of the
present owner of the house

The Glasgow Style

The Glasgow Style

Elizabeth Cumming

Yet the essence of the Glasgow group [...] rests in an underlying emotional and poetical quality. It seeks a highly charged artistic atmosphere or more specifically an atmosphere of a mystical, symbolic kind [...]. The special character of the Mackintosh group rests as much in form, especially in their ideas about the relationship between surface and decoration, as in colour [...] one may say that the Glaswegians have borrowed the idea that Whistler introduced into painting for the decoration of their rooms [...].[1]

In his commentary on contemporary British domestic architecture, *Das englische Haus*, first published in Berlin in 1904-05, Hermann Muthesius (1861-1927) singled Glasgow out for praise. Much of the book was devoted to the Arts and Crafts movement and its two basic tenets, respect for tradition and functionalism. According to Muthesius, Scots designers, and especially those practising in Glasgow, had digested many of the inventive ideas of the English movement, most especially the unified artistic interior. Visually sophisticated Glaswegians (most notably Charles Rennie Mackintosh) avoided both the clutter of the English interior and the excessive precision espoused by such architects as C.F.A. Voysey. Indeed, Muthesius thought that around the turn of the century the Glasgow movement was not only peripheral but in many respects antithetical to the Arts and Crafts movement itself:

The Scottish movement is a reaction against the insistent utilitarian and rational principles of the Arts and Crafts camp in London. They preached death to romanticism and were thinking mainly of the stylistic chaos, the meaningless ornament and the forgotten considerations of material and craftsmanship that marked the art of the nineteenth century. The Scots replied that without imagination there is no art. Here again are the two poles of realism and idealism between which a developing art vacillates so freely. Realism is the refreshing dip which is salutary from time to time if art is to remain in touch with the world, to keep its feet on the ground. But the ultimate goal of art can never be other than idealistic [...].[2]

Muthesius's view of Glasgow design raises several questions. Did it really run against the tide of Arts and Crafts belief and practise? If the work emanating from Glasgow was indeed so alien to the British movement, did Glaswegian designers see their work as Scots or European? And how did other 'outsiders' view them? Was Mackintosh really the pivotal figure in Glasgow design or were there others to whom at least as much credit should be given? And lastly, given the fact that Glasgow design was primarily artistic, what role did manufacturers and patrons play in its progress? Only by surveying Glasgow design between 1880 and 1914 can we attempt to answer these questions.

Education and modern design

When, in 1885, at the age of thirty-two, Francis Henry Newbery (fig. 3.1 and cat. 17) assumed his post as headmaster of the Glasgow School of Art and Haldane Academy (as the institution was called between 1869 and 1892), it was located in the same block on Sauchiehall Street as the Corporation Art Gallery. Like other Schools of Design, Glasgow's was governed and financed from London under the 'South Kensington' system, whereby its share of governmental resources was allocated in accordance with its performance in national competitions. Under the direction of Thomas Symonds, Glasgow already ranked third among British schools, following Birmingham and Lambeth.[3]

Newbery was no stranger to the British system of art education, having served on the staff of the Art Training Schools in South Kensington. He soon gained the confidence of the Glasgow board and was determined to reform Scottish design. First of all, he wanted to raise the standards of commercial design, to which end he invited William Morris, father of the Arts and Crafts movement, to address public meetings in Glasgow. Secondly, Newbery affirmed John Ruskin's belief, elaborated by Morris in the 1870s and 1880s, that if an object were designed and executed with pleasure, it would be intrinsically beautiful.

Acting on the assumption that such events were essential to progress in industrial design, Newbery helped organise the first Glasgow International Exhibition in 1888, three years after his arrival in the

3.1 Maurice Greiffenhagen, Fra Newbery, 1913 (Glasgow Museums and Art Galleries) cat. 17

city. The Exhibition gave local manufacturers the opportunity to present their wares to the west of Scotland. It attracted no fewer than five million seven hundred thousand people, outstripping the Colonial and Indian Exhibitions held in London and Edinburgh respectively in 1886. Mounted in Kelvingrove Park, the Glasgow extravaganza combined historical displays, trade stalls and exotic oriental architecture designed by James Sellars.[4] 'Baghdad by Kelvinside', as it was popularly known, was a curious blend of Byzantine, Moorish and Indian-style temporary structures.[5] The main building housed displays of fine and applied art, including one hundred and seventy modern sculptures chosen by Newbery that, like some of the other sections of the International Exhibition, were intended not only to entertain visitors but also to inspire local talent. The arches and pendentives of the main building's large central dome were inscribed with texts and painted with four allegorical figures representing Art, Industry, Agriculture and Science by Guthrie, Henry, Walton and Lavery.[6]

Francis Newbery - known to friends, colleagues and students as 'Fra' - was as much a socialist, idealist and teacher as an administrator. In the early 1890s he became a leading exponent of educational reforms that were to affect most art and design schools in Britain. By this time design and the applied arts had achieved both a popular and professional status beyond all expectations. In London the Art Workers' Guild, founded in 1884, had been striving to equalise the status of architecture, art and design. The new Arts and Crafts Exhibition Society started showing a wide variety of both manufactured and crafted goods in 1888. Other cities followed suit by establishing organisations devoted to the exhibition of both fine and applied arts, such as the Society of Scottish Artists, founded in Edinburgh in 1891. To stimulate local design further, Newbery arranged for a group of objects that had been shown in London by the Arts and Crafts Exhibitions Society in the autumn of 1889 to be transferred to the galleries next door to his School of Art in January 1890. The objects included textiles, furniture and metalwork designed by Voysey, Morris and Walter Crane, among others. Newbery was already acquainted with many leaders of the Society, and encouraged Crane and Lewis F. Day, as well as Morris, to speak at the School in the late 1880s and early 1890s.

Exhibitions and guilds provided a marketplace as well as opportunities for trade and craft to mix and new partnerships to form. But the method of training new members of the profession had to be reformed. The Technical Instruction Act of 1889 authorised local authorities to raise taxes by one penny for the sake of technical education, but most school directors agreed that not only more money but also a new approach was needed. They affirmed Morris and Ruskin's conviction that South Kensington stifled

creativity, and argued that architects, designers and artisans could and should work together in harmony. Between 1890 and 1910, therefore, from such British cities as Birmingham, Liverpool, Leicester and London, to Dublin, Dundee, Edinburgh and Glasgow, technical training was radically reformed.[7]

The first thing that happened in Glasgow was that the Technical Art Studios were established in the summer of 1892. According to a contemporary source, the Studios were 'to offer a complete cycle of Technical Artistic Education applicable to the Industrial Arts of the City of Glasgow'.[8] As at other institutions of its kind, the classes were taught by local artist-craftsmen.[9] The new craft classes offered by the Technical Art Studios - such as woodcarving, gesso, repoussé metalwork, leatherwork and bookbinding - were only open to students who had already completed the course in design and decorative art at the School. The name 'Technical Art Studios' was important to Newbery, for it emphasized the union of craftsmanship and design. Especially from the mid-1890s, the curriculum was based on what his wife Jessie Newbery called 'the sum of tradition',[10] that is the conscious and unconscious appreciation of indigenous culture. Given this balance between design and craftsmanship, Newbery believed the right student could arrive at radical new design ideas far beyond technical perfection or artistic inspiration.

The Glasgow School of Art most closely resembled that of the new Central School of Arts and Crafts in London. Founded in Regent Street in 1896, the Central School was co-directed by the architect and writer William Richard Lethaby and the sculptor George Frampton. As educational theorists, Lethaby and Newbery had much in common: they both believed workshops, not classrooms, were the best context for learning, and that practical experiment was the most effective method of teaching. Lethaby always emphasized the importance of learning design and craft by practising them. Like Morris, he likened craft and design to cooking:

Art is not a special sauce applied to ordinary cooking: it is the cooking itself if it is good. Most simply and generally art may be thought of as the well doing of what needs doing. *Every work of art shows that it was made by a human being for a human being [...]. Art is the humanity put into workmanship, the rest is slavery [...].*[11]

One course Newbery introduced in Glasgow - 'designing in the material' - placed the greatest emphasis on craft. Yet neither he nor his London colleague Lethaby rejected mechanisation. As design school administrators they could not have done so in any case: they were responsible for training designers to work in an industrial society.[12] Indeed the Glasgow School of Art had been founded 'with a

view to the improvement of [...] National Manufactures', and as early as the 1840s textile manufacturers in the west of Scotland had pressed for a school of design to train both male and female artisans to enhance their competitiveness vis-à-vis France in particular.

Newbery and Lethaby both saw handcraft as desirable, indeed essential, within a world dominated by national economies and commerce. They sought to provide a broad education that developed skills and bred an understanding of profitable relations among the crafts on the one hand, and between them and industry on the other. For Lethaby, in particular, the key to educational success lay in recruiting teachers with the right experience: among others he employed the enamellist Alexander Fisher, the bookbinder Douglas Cockerell, the architect Halsey Ricardo, the amateur calligrapher Edward Johnston, and the stained-glass designer Christopher Whall, all important London-based figures in the history of the Arts and Crafts movement. Both schools relied heavily on visiting lecturers drawn from the cream of professional practitioners, especially architects.

The Glasgow Style

The new approach to artistic training had a direct impact on the daily life of each city in the mid-1890s. The equality of craft with art and art with industry which was preached by the Glasgow School led to the establishment of a number of workshops by young artists after they had finished their studies. Among the artists were the sisters Margaret and Frances Macdonald, Margaret and Marion Wilson, and Margaret and Mary Gilmour. Small businesses of this kind afforded young, unmarried women a degree of financial and professional independence that was hitherto unknown.

Throughout the 1890s Glasgow was at the forefront of the Arts and Crafts movement in Britain. According to Hermann Muthesius, however, the English rejected the 'highly charged artistic atmosphere' of work from Glasgow, and especially that of 'The Four' - Charles Rennie Mackintosh, James Herbert MacNair and the Macdonald sisters - at the 1896 Arts and Crafts Exhibition Society. Nor were The Four the only Glasgow designers singled out for criticism in London: the journal *The Studio* found the work of still other alumni of the School of Art, such as the illustrator and craftworker Jessie M. King, equally unacceptable. One correspondent placed the blame for King's design squarely on her training.[13] Newbery's support of the professional and corresponding rejection of the amateur - that aesthetic 'dilettante young lady who would decorate tambourines and milking stools with impossible forget-me-knots and sunflowers'[14] - and his commitment to freedom and innovation in both art and design, were ideals shared by the entire teaching staff, many of whom were former students. Especially prominent among them was Jessie Newbery, who reorganised the art needlework classes in 1894 and also taught mosaic in 1896-98, enamelling in 1895-99 and book decoration in 1899.[15] Jessie Newbery also showed her own work, at for instance the Arts and Crafts Exhibition Society in 1896. Though her teaching methods and work were progressive - she introduced simple patterns and inexpensive, natural materials to hand embroidery (fig. 3.2 and cat. 104) - she was also a theorist who helped advance contemporary Glasgow opinion. Like her husband, Jessie Newbery believed in the pursuit of excellence and the universality of good design:

I believe that the greatest thing in the world is for a man to know that he is his own, and that the great end in art is the discovery of the self of the artist. I believe in being the sum of tradition; that consciously or unconsciously men are all so, but some are more derivative than others. I believe in education consisting of seeing the best that has been done. Then, having this high standard thus set before us, in doing what we like to do: that for our fathers, this for us. I believe that nothing is common or unclean; that the design and decoration of a pepper pot is as important, in its degree, as the conception of a cathedral. I believe that material, space, and consequent use discover their own exigences and as such have to be considered well.[16]

Gleeson White, editor of *The Studio*, published this credo in 1897, in his third article on 'Some Glasgow Designers and their Work'. One of the points he made was that Jessie Newbery touched on 'far more important matters than mere needlework' and seemed 'to state not infelicitously the guiding principles of many a designer today'. A Londoner who believed the Glasgow School was at the forefront of British design, White wrote 'that for all its waywardness it has a firm hold of beauty, and is striving to make beautiful harmonies of colour, and beautiful combinations of line'. Commenting specifically on Jessie Newbery's embroideries, he added that 'they decorate not merely the surface to which they are applied, but also form most pleasant spots or ornament in the larger scheme of decoration of any room where they happen to be placed'.

White recognised that there was a special relationship between objects and architectural design in Glasgow when he devoted his first article to 'The Four'. Since the expanding School of Art needed more space, its governors announced a competition for a new building in 1896. The entry submitted by the local architectural firm of Honeyman & Keppie, designed by Charles Rennie Mackintosh, finally won. By the time the building started going up in Renfrew Street in 1897, Glasgow design had its own distinct, progressive identity, distinguished by 'material, space

3.3 *Glasgow School of Art, designed by Charles Rennie Mackintosh in 1896, 1906, built 1897-99, 1907-09. Photograph by Brian and Shere c. 1955, courtesy of Glasgow School of Art*

and consequent use', according to Jessie Newbery, or in the words of Hermann Muthesius, by 'form and relationship between surface and decoration'. This applied equally to the School of Art's new home and the work its students produced. To contain costs the School's governors had declared they wanted a 'plain building'. The final result, constructed in 1897-99 and 1907-09, has been justly proclaimed Mackintosh's 'masterwork' (fig. 3.3).[17] Like Glasgow design generally, it was a deceptively simple, practical structure, rich in organic symbolism and traditional Scots form.

The Glasgow tea room

Winning the School competition placed Mackintosh at the forefront of Glasgow architectural design. Yet even in 1897 he was an odd man out: most Glasgow architects designed neither objects nor complete interiors and few designers (with the exception of MacNair) had Mackintosh's architectural training. Had Gleeson White not died in 1898, he would have devoted an entire article in *The Studio* to George Walton, a designer who was more characteristic of the city's designers in many ways. A year older than Mackintosh, Walton was the younger brother of the painter Ernest Arthur Walton, of Helen Walton, and of Hannah Walton. In 1888 Catherine Cranston commissioned Walton, a bank clerk who had

attended evening classes at the School of Art, to redecorate her Crown Tea Rooms in Argyle Street, first opened ten years earlier. At the Crown he employed an Aesthetic style of wall stencilling based on stylised leaves and roses. Having established himself as an ecclesiastical and residential decorator, Walton soon received a number of other commissions, including the decoration of Miss Cranston's new suite of tea rooms in Buchanan Street. These rooms (1896-97) were Walton's most important contribution to Glasgow design for, in combining an elegant simplicity of form with exciting materials and colour, they bridged the gap between the Aesthetic movement and the new Glasgow Arts and Crafts design. The Billiard Room had a sturdy, simple table with buttress-shaped legs, chairs with solid curved arms that seemed to embrace their occupants and, for glamour, a painted 'medieval' frieze of a forest filled with animals, birds and hunters. Both the backs of chairs and the large fireplace were decorated with a flattened heart motif which, in a social meeting place, betokened welcome. It soon became the designer's trademark.

The Buchanan Street Tea Rooms broke new ground thanks to the fact that Walton commissioned Mackintosh to design stencils for the walls (fig. 3.4). For the Ladies' Tea Room Mackintosh developed the symbolic female figure in his drawing *Part Seen, Imagined Part* of April 1896 into a lifesize pattern that ran in pairs along either side of a stylised tree. Dressed in white, each with a golden nimbus, and wreathed by stylised plant tendrils - Muthesius's 'strange tangle of lines in the figural compositions' - these figures formed a strong, contrasting background to Walton's traditional ladder-backed chairs. In the Luncheon Room, Mackintosh used equally stylised motifs of trees and peacocks. Each room was designed as an experience in colour and form. Every detail, down to the cutlery and the uniforms of the staff, was fashioned specifically for each room. Together with the sexual contrast between the design of the various tea, luncheon and dining rooms, this helped create tremendous diversity, which caught the public's imagination. As the local newspaper *St Mungo* reported:

The latest addition to Glasgow tea-rooms has all the aesthetic wrinkles brought to perfection. The male attendants are clothed in vestments of quaint and soothing design, the man who works the elevator being a veritable poem. Even the spoons are fashioned upon a pattern that will thrill with ecstasy the souls of willow-pattern and the sunflower brigade [...].[18]

The response of Arts and Crafts designers and commentators outside the city was somewhat less enthusiastic. Gleeson White called the Tea Rooms an 'honest attempt at novelty'. After visiting them with James Guthrie, the English architect Edwin Lutyens described them in a letter to his fiancée:

[...] all is curiously painted and coloured [...]. Some of the knives are purple and are put as spots of colour! It is all quite good, all just a little outré, *a thing we must avoid [...].*[19]

3.4 *The Ladies' Tea Room, Buchanan Street Tea Rooms, Glasgow, 1896-97. Photograph courtesy of the Annan Collection, Glasgow*

Miss Cranston's Argyle Street Tea Rooms, likewise designed by Walton and Mackintosh, opened in 1897. Mackintosh was in control of this project. His solid oak chairs and tables, which dominated the spaces and created a crisper, reductionist effect, contrasted with Walton's daintily stencilled walls. As Roger Billcliffe has pointed out, the furniture was unexceptional Arts and Crafts on the whole, save for the high-backed chairs with pierced oval back-rails. The chairs may have been heightened on account of the wall partitions, beams and columns, which dominated the space.

Mackintosh and Modernism

After 1897 Mackintosh became Miss Cranston's sole architect and designer, providing her with tea rooms and, from 1904, interiors for her own home, 'Hous'hill'. The Ingram Street rooms (1900, 1907, 1911) and the Willow Tea Rooms (1903, 1917), together with the School of Art, form his major contributions to the design of public interiors. After Mackintosh married Margaret Macdonald in 1900 he achieved a synthesis of art, craft and architecture. In the 1890s, Margaret and her sister Frances had both worked in repoussé brass and lead, and surrounded their watercolours with lead frames. Margaret's use of handcrafted details such as gesso, beaten metalwork and stained-glass panels in interiors remained faithful to the Glasgow Arts and Crafts movement.

The first of the Ingram Street rooms - the White Dining Room (1900) - had woodwork painted white, including screens, and two large gesso panels by Margaret and her husband (fig. 3.5). The White Dining Room furniture was formal: rigidly geometric, its overall severity was only partly relieved by the pierced backs of the taller chairs (fig. 3.6 and cat. 89). In the Willow Tea Rooms on Sauchiehall Street (1903) Mackintosh created a series of interrelated spaces that rank among the most thrilling Scottish interiors of the early twentieth century. Outside Mackintosh totally ignored the building's surroundings, while inside he used screens and high-backed chairs to articulate the space and to divide it horizontally and vertically. The building and its furnishings most closely resemble the rationalised designs of the English architect-designer of the Aesthetic movement, E.W. Godwin, who, according to *The British Architect* in 1878, had urged architects to be 'independent of fashions by simply being architects and artists, taking up work and doing it as their own'.[20] In a lecture entitled 'Seemliness', Mackintosh advised his contemporaries to *[...] go your own way and let your neighbour go his [...]. Don't meddle with other peoples* [sic] *ideas [...]. Shake off all the props - the props tradition and authority offer you.*[21]

Yet, for all his talk of purifying architecture and

3.5 *Charles Rennie Mackintosh (designer), The White Dining Room, Ingram Street Tea Rooms, 1900. Photograph courtesy of the Hunterian Art Gallery, University of Glasgow, Mackintosh Collection*

3.6 *Charles Rennie Mackintosh (designer), Chair for the Ingram Street Tea Rooms (Glasgow Museums and Art Galleries) cat. 89*

past for solutions was considered antithetical to the Modernist ideal.

Pamela Robertson recently discussed the complexity of Mackintosh's loyalty both to Modernism and to Arts and Crafts, and the extent to which he was influenced by Ruskin and the architect-theorists J.D. Sedding, Lethaby and Godwin,[22] with whom he shared such ideals as a 'commune of all the crafts' where 'all arts were united in one building'.[23] He planned his buildings with the greatest attention to detail and, in the case of the private houses designed after 1899, often incorporated Margaret's ideas for textiles and gesso panels. For some, including even Muthesius, their interiors were simply too intense for comfort, which (together with Mackintosh's highmindedness) doubtless alienated many potential patrons. In a famous passage in *Das englische Haus*, Muthesius commented that

Mackintosh's rooms are refined to a degree which the lives of even the artistically educated are still a long way from matching. The delicacy and austerity of their artistic atmosphere would tolerate no admixture of the ordinariness which fills our lives. Even a book in an unsuitable binding would disturb the atmosphere simply by lying on the table, indeed even the man or woman of today - especially the man in his unadorned working attire - treads like a stranger in this fairy-tale world.[24]

A clue to the understanding of Mackintosh's philosophy after 1900 lies in Sedding's well-known anti-historicist aphorism, 'There is hope in honest error, none in the icy perfections of the mere stylist'. These words had tremendous meaning for a whole generation of Arts and Crafts architects and one known to have been copied out by Mackintosh himself in 1892 and 1901 (fig. 3.8). But after the turn of the century Modernists no longer despised the term 'perfection' or even 'icy', which could signify a truth just as deep as the organic ideology of the Arts and Crafts movement. In a return to Apollonian values, the 'gothic' - that is, the natural, the linear, the emotional, the honest - was superseded by the 'classical' - the formal, the solid, the perfect. By 1905 the vegetable motifs on Mackintosh's furniture and walls had been replaced by uncompromisingly pure form. Rational formality was certainly nothing new to Mackintosh, even in his decorative work in two dimensions. The full-length repeated stencilled figures at the Buchanan Street Ladies' Tea Room, for instance, had been essentially hieratical, almost Byzantine, but few other British architects took such an obvious step in that direction.

Ever a perfectionist, Mackintosh's relationship with his clients, for example with the Governors of the Glasgow School of Art, could be difficult. Like the architect and designer M.H. Baillie Scott, he took a holistic approach to architecture. The many

abandoning tradition, in practice Mackintosh relied heavily on the past. The references both Mackintoshes made to it were as intellectual as they were visual. The jewel-like Ladies' Room, or Room de Luxe, at the heart of the Willow Tea Rooms, with its tall chairs painted silver, leaded mirror-glass, stretched silk panelling and Margaret's gesso panel, *Willowwood* - based on a sonnet sequence in Dante Gabriel Rossetti's *House of Life* - was both sophisticated and Aesthetic, but its 'Willow' theme - 'Sauchiehall' in Scots means 'alley of the willows' - gave it a precise, local context (fig. 3.7). The room was deliberately feminine, surrounded by more masculine, almost old-fashioned Arts and Crafts rooms that catered to a mixed clientèle, and were furnished with tall ladder-backed and squat, club-like chairs, thus creating a contrast between the spiritual and the mundane.

The Mackintoshes' ambivalence about two sets of values - the aesthetic and the practical, the linear and the spatial, the masculine and the feminine - was an essential aspect of the dialogue between the Arts and Crafts movement and Modernism in Britain around 1900. In the work of most Scots designers, including Mackintosh, the two were tightly interwoven; casting them as polarities, that is Realism and Idealism, as Muthesius did, misconstrued the basic tenets of both. When it came to architecture, after all, exponents of the Arts and Crafts movement and Modernists were both pragmatic; they subordinated form to function. It was with respect to the past that English designers most obviously differed from their Scots counterparts. Around the turn of the century, Scots designers of both persuasions commonly synthesised past and present, whereas in England, plumbing the

3.7 Charles Rennie Mackintosh (designer), The Ladies' Room, or Room de Luxe, Willow Tea Rooms, Sauchiehall Street, 1903. Photograph courtesy of the Hunterian Art Gallery, University of Glasgow, Mackintosh Collection

functional aspects of his architecture notwithstanding, he was by nature an 'art architect' whose primary interest was design. By the same token, his furniture evinces little interest in craftsmanship; indeed he sometimes ignored the advice on structural improvements he received.

Manufacture in Glasgow

More so than Mackintosh, George Walton exemplifies the versatile, almost opportunist, character of the turn-of-the-century Glasgow designer. Like other Glasgow artists and designers he benefited from the building boom in the late 1880s and 1890s by diversifying into a number of decorative media. Glasgow architects wanted to introduce stained glass and painted tiles to all levels of housing, from tenement blocks of flats to large detached houses. These years witnessed the corresponding growth of 'art' companies such as J. & W. Guthrie and William Meikle & Company.[25] Artists like James Guthrie (no relation), David Gauld and Harrington Mann designed for stained or painted glass, the decorative art most closely related to their own craft. J. & W. Guthrie was one of the firms that produced their designs. James Guthrie's earliest known piece was designed in 1887 for the home of

3.8 Charles Rennie Mackintosh, There is hope in honest error, none in the icy perfections of the mere stylist, 1901. Mackintosh also lettered the text in German. Both were published in Rudolph von Larisch, Beispiele Künstlerischer Schrift, Vienna 1902. Photograph courtesy of the Hunterian Art Gallery, University of Glasgow, Mackintosh Collection

the Glasgow carpet king, James Templeton, on the Clyde. Gauld and Mann, who shared a St Vincent Place studio between 1891-94, designed for the firm throughout most of the decade. Walton had likewise broadened his design career: from stencilled wallpaper he turned to light fixtures, painted tiles, glass and furniture. His early patrons included William Burrell, for whose house he designed stained glass in 1892 (fig 3.9, p. 100). Walton's work in stained and table glass had the widest circulation: many of his door and screen panels made popular by the Argyle Tea Rooms were manufactured by James Benson of the Blythswood Stained Glass Company, one of several ecclesiastical glass-makers who thrived in the city centre, while his table glass was manufactured by James Couper & Sons, an enterprising firm who employed designs by Christopher Dresser in their 'Clutha' range between approximately 1880 and 1896.[26]

Of the many Glasgow firms who successfully bridged art and industry, J. & W. Guthrie was one of the most important. John Guthrie had received his design training at the Haldane Academy and, in partnership with his brother William from 1874, expanded the family decorating and furnishing firm, founded in Glasgow in 1852 in the wake of London's Great Exhibition. By the 1890s they had a London showroom and were 'house and church decorators and artists in stained glass (domestic and ecclesiological), plain and ornamental glaziers, art furnishers, and dealers in antique furniture'. This innovative firm exhibited not only at trade fairs but also at the Arts and Crafts Exhibition Society in London and at the International Exhibitions in Paris in 1900 and in Glasgow 1901. John Guthrie, a member of the Art Workers' Guild in London, was committed to education: he was superintendent of the School of Art's Technical Studios from 1900 until 1903, shortly after the firm had expanded to become J. & W. Guthrie and Andrew Wells Ltd. The company played an important role in the development of progressive Glasgow design not only because of its stained glass workshops, which employed the cream of British designers in the craft such as Christopher Whall and Robert Anning Bell, but also because of their furniture and decorating studios, which made and retailed furniture by Mackintosh from 1894 and executed most of the stencilled decorations for Miss Cranston's tea rooms and Mackintosh's Hill House in 1903. For Mackintosh and Walton, working with the firm Guthrie & Wells was the nearest they would come to an Arts and Crafts partnership with a guild of handicraft.

By the mid-1890s Walton (soon followed by Mackintosh) was winning contracts outside Scotland. In 1896 the chocolate manufacturers Rowntree commissioned him to decorate their Scarborough tea rooms, and the following year he was asked to design

3.10 E.A. Taylor (designer), Drawing Room, Wylie & Lochhead Pavilion, 1901 Glasgow International Exhibition. Photograph Glasgow Museums and Art Galleries

the exhibition of the Royal Photographic Society in London, where he settled. For William Davidson, head of Kodak's European sales division, he furnished Kodak shops in Britain and the rest of Europe, and also designed architecture. One of the houses Walton designed for Davidson, 'The Leys' at Elstree, was liberally illustrated in *Das englische Haus*. In contrast to houses by Mackintosh, these remained wholly within the Arts and Crafts tradition, and more closely resembled the work of Baillie Scott than that of any Scots architect.

In his role as Glasgow's most innovative architect-designer, Charles Rennie Mackintosh served, indirectly, as a catalyst in Glasgow. His School of Art and tea rooms helped cultivate the public's taste for the avant-garde. By the late 1890s local manufacturers were hiring other progressive Glasgow designers to meet the growing demand for avant-garde furniture on the part of the middle class. Of these, Walton, George Logan, John Ednie and E.A. Taylor were the most renowned. Around 1900 they were designing elegant, reductionist furniture which, though it shared the spatial qualities of Mackintosh's work, also reflected current British interest in late eighteenth-century architecture and design.[27] The work of these men was distinguished by clean-cut forms, handsome proportions and attention to detail. The wood they used was either painted or chosen for its fine grain; their metalwork and furniture might be inlaid with mother-of-pearl, enamel, or even semi-precious stones; their textiles and stained-glass panels fitted into cupboard doors and walls. The same attitude shaped the elegant book covers and interiors designed by Talwin Morris, art director of the international Glasgow-based publishers Blackie and Sons. These finely crafted, manufactured objects, like so much of what the Glasgow School produced, added a touch of luxury to the Scottish middle-class interior.

The furniture manufacturing and retailing firm of

3.11 George Logan (designer), Rossetti Library, Wylie & Lochhead Pavilion, 1901 Glasgow International Exhibition. Photograph Glasgow Museums and Art Galleries

Wylie & Lochhead, in association with the School of Art, was largely responsible for popularising the Glasgow Style.[28] The company was the Glasgow equivalent of the London retailers and manufacturers Liberty & Company, which catered to the new and relatively affluent middle class. Like Liberty & Company, Wylie & Lochhead developed a popular (yet relatively expensive) version of Arts and Crafts design that took its place in their shops in Glasgow alongside more traditional historicist lines such as Renaissance, Jacobean and Hepplewhite. Around the turn of the century Wylie & Lochhead sensed that Mackintosh's new Art School and the Cranston tea rooms had influenced popular taste. Like the carpet and textile manufacturers Templetons in Glasgow, or Alexander Morton & Co. in Darvel, Ayrshire, Wylie & Lochhead also exploited the latest technological advances.

A redefinition of form and proportion was not the Glasgow stylists' only contribution. They believed interesting ranges and combinations of textures and colours were at least as important, and that objects should be 'beautiful, pleasant, and if need be, useful'.[29] Jessie Newbery, for instance, affirmed the 'opposition of straight lines to curved; of horizontal to vertical; of purple to green, and green to blue'.[30] As evidenced by the present exhibition, Glasgow design was dominated by shades of purple, pink, silver and green. Colour was not to be confined to fabrics, but should help define furniture, doors, ceilings and walls. A furnished room, the designers believed, was no less than a three-dimensional work of art: not surprisingly, therefore, their colours were more attuned to the soft-toned paintings of Whistler and the Hague School - to nature itself, in effect - than the vibrant hues generally favoured by British textile designers. The Wylie & Lochhead pavilion at the 1901 Glasgow International Exhibition had rooms designed by three Glaswegians, namely George Logan, E.A. Taylor and John Ednie. In terms of colour, Taylor's drawing room was considered the most daring: the furniture (cat. 110, 111) was stained purple, inlaid with mother-of-pearl butterflies and set against a pale green silk wallcovering, white painted woodwork and a carpet of stronger green (fig 3.10). Though the colour combination - which corresponded with the thistle, Scotland's national emblem - was popular in Glasgow, critics elsewhere were less enthusiastic: one of them scorned the 'washed out secondary colours [which] clang on the optic nerve'.[31] Logan also used a great deal of green; his Rossetti Library in the pavilion included a frieze of birds and trees and a carpet of stylised roses and leaves (fig. 3.11).

Glasgow in Europe

By the early 1900s Glasgow design was being seen not only in Arts and Crafts exhibitions within Britain - organised by the Arts and Crafts Exhibition Society in London, the Society of Scottish Artists in Edinburgh, and two Glasgow-based societies founded in 1898, the Scottish Guild of Handicraft and the Scottish Society of Art Workers - but also in international exhibitions abroad. The reputation Glasgow design achieved in Europe between 1900 and 1904 was almost entirely thanks to Fra Newbery and Charles Rennie Mackintosh.

There were two reasons for promoting British (and specifically Glaswegian) products abroad in the 1900s. Firstly, in Britain as in Germany progress in the field of design was automatically associated with economic prosperity. Taking Glasgow's manufactures abroad was tantamount to broadcasting the city's wealth: it told the world that by amalgamating art and industry, the Second City of the Empire had raised design standards to new heights. Glasgow's strategy was particularly evident at the Turin International Exhibition of Decorative Art and, to a lesser extent, at the Venice Biennale of 1899. Secondly, the Arts and Crafts movement, in which Glasgow figured prominently, was now on the cutting edge of European design. At a time when the workshop was such an important part of the manufacturing process, the Glasgow School of Art showed how craft and mass-production could happily co-exist.

Glasgow also contributed to the idealist side of the European Arts and Crafts movement. The city's designers were acutely aware of their Celtic heritage. This was considered especially important in an age of romantic nationalism, when other countries on the fringes of Europe such as Sweden and Hungary were anxious to revive their native crafts. Those countries admired the writings of Ruskin and Morris, not only for their enthusiasm about indigenous crafts but also for the role they ascribed to artists and craftworkers in reforming society. As the British Arts and Crafts movement itself was stimulated by crafts from non-industrialised countries, so developing European nations looked for inspiration to Britain, the source and still the heart of the movement, in their quest for cultural regeneration. Scotland, and Glasgow in particular, served as a rich model.

In 1902 the entire Wylie & Lochhead's 1901 pavilion was taken to the Iparművészeti Museum in Budapest as part of an exhibition of British Arts and Crafts selected by a committee of eight that included Crane, James Paton (director of the new Glasgow Art Galleries at Kelvingrove) and Newbery.[32] Though a number of pieces, including Wylie & Lochhead work, were purchased by the Museum, on the whole Glasgow work was not well received. It may have been simply too artistic and self-conscious.[33] Newbery was involved in a second exhibition mounted in Europe in 1902: the International Exhibition of Modern Decorative Art. In contrast to the Budapest Exhibition, that in Turin was consciously design-oriented. Mackintosh, who had visited the city with Newbery in April, was the official designer of the three rooms allocated to the Scots. Of these, the largest was painted purple and white and housed work representing the Glasgow School of Art and other Scottish Arts and Crafts. For this room Mackintosh provided tall stencilled banners and wooden box stalls based on his design for the School of Art display at the 1901 Glasgow International Exhibition. The other two rooms - the one coloured white, silver and pink, the other grey, gold and white - were used by the Mackintoshes and the MacNairs as settings for their own work. The 'Rose Boudoir', the Mackintoshes' room, contained watercolours, glass and beaten metalwork panels, electric lamps, furniture painted white, black or green and some set with gesso panels or stencilled canvas, and last but not least, three gesso panels by Margaret Macdonald Mackintosh on the theme of the rose.

Fra Newbery's contributions to exhibitions abroad served to contextualise Glasgow design and extend the city's already considerable reputation. In the 1890s, long before the second Glasgow International Exhibition of 1901 and before Muthesius wrote his book, Glasgow was already known in Europe as a lively centre of the visual arts. In its early stages Mackintosh's happy relations with European designers was partly due to the success of the 'Glasgow Boys' and supports a general case for 1900 Glasgow art and design to be considered as Scottish and European but not British. Over one thousand paintings by the Glasgow School and their followers had been shown at the Munich Secession or Art Society by 1900 and a good number were bought by state galleries throughout Germany. Thirteen

'Boys' were elected corresponding members of the Munich Secession in 1893 and Lavery joined the Secessions of Munich, Berlin and Vienna.[34] When the Vienna Secession held its inaugural exhibition in its new building, Olbrich's 'Golden Cabbage', in 1898, several Glaswegians contributed, including E.A. Walton, William Strang and Lavery. The following year paintings by Crawhall, Whitelaw Hamilton, Hornel, Kennedy, MacNicol, Mann, Gauld, and Macaulay Stevenson were included.

Gleeson White's three articles on 'Some Glasgow Designers and their Work' had an extraordinarily wide circulation across Germany and Austria where there was already widespread admiration for the ideology of the British Arts and Crafts movement, especially for its designers' dedication to collective design, the *Gesamtkunstwerk*. The October 1897 issue of *The Studio*, which publicised Jessie Newbery's (and Glasgow's) creed for the applied arts, also included an article on Ashbee's Guild of Handcraft and an advertisement placed by F. Brückmann of Munich for his 'Dekorative Kunst, a new German illustrated monthly'. Brückmann, Mackintosh's first foreign client, was thus in touch with British design, and, as Roger Billcliffe has pointed out, probably commissioned furniture for his dining room from Mackintosh as a direct result of the first of White's articles.[35] The Brückmann pieces, with their beaten metalwork and stained-glass door panels, set in natural, waxed oak, are among the last of Mackintosh's wholehearted Arts and Crafts designs.

Brückmann's support and his publications of Mackintosh's work in *Dekorative Kunst* in 1898 did much to publicise his designs in both Germany and Austria. In the autumn of 1900, the Mackintoshes and the MacNairs were invited to contribute a room

to the eighth Vienna Secession to be held that November. The organisers of the show, designers Josef Hoffmann and Koloman Moser with Felician von Myrbach, director of the Kunstgewerbeschule, wanted to bring together some of the most interesting current work from across Europe. They also commissioned displays by the *Maison Moderne* from Paris and Ashbee's Guild. Both the rooms furnished by the guild and 'The Four' deeply impressed Viennese designers and critics. Guild furniture seemed as 'if they came from a rectangular planet [...] everything vertical, at right angles [...]'.[36] Simplicity dominated the Mackintosh group's Room X, where walls and woodwork were painted white to offset two large gesso panels, *The Wassail* by Mackintosh and *The May Queen* by Margaret (fig. 3.12). Both panels had been commissioned for the Ingram Street Tea Rooms. In fact the theme of Room X was 'A Tea Room' but it was furnished in a manner closer to the Mackintoshes' home in Glasgow: with the exhibition arranged at such short notice, most of the furniture came from their flat at 120 Mains Street. The only other known pieces were a beaten metalwork clock by Margaret and Frances, and a wall cabinet and framed book illustrations by Frances and Herbert MacNair. In its subtle balance between delicacy and strength in both colour and design, the room must have harmonised well with the white, green and gold exterior of the Secession building. It had an astonishing influence on 1900s Viennese design, especially mural decoration, the most important example of which was Gustav Klimt's Beethoven frieze for the fourteenth Secession (1902), today partly restored in the basement gallery of Olbrich's building.[37]

Mackintosh's impact on Vienna was not confined to a single exhibition. Fritz Wärndorfer - 'a man of culture with a leaning towards modern art, and a capitalist to boot'[38] - had visited Mackintosh earlier in 1900 and, sometime between late 1900 and the spring of 1902, commissioned a music room for his house in Vienna; the critic Ludwig Hevesi described the room as 'a place of spiritual joy'.[39] The Wärndorfer music salon was a luxurious version of the Secession display, incorporating a piano fitted with two gesso panels by Margaret on the theme of sound, or music, in nature: *The Opera of the Wind* and *The Opera of the Sea*. Three more of her gesso panels, illustrating Maeterlinck's *The Seven Princesses*, were probably executed in 1906. In its design unity and layout, especially in its cosy inglenook, the Mackintoshes' square room spoke the language of Arts and Crafts. Furthermore, the combination of feminine furniture painted white and crafts techniques such as stencilling on chair backs, showed continuity with, not rejection of, British Arts and Crafts ideals. As yet there was no trace of incipient Modernism. The delicacy of the room closely resembled Mackintosh's 1901-02 designs for Mrs Rowat, Jessie Newbery's mother

3.12 *Detail of Room X at the Eighth Vienna Secession, 1900, showing a detail from the gesso panel* The May Queen *(1900) and an embroidered hanging by Margaret Macdonald Mackintosh, as well as a cheval mirror painted white (1900) and a chair with a pierced oval back rail (1897) by Charles Rennie Mackintosh from their Glasgow flat at 120 Mains Street. The photograph was published in Vienna in* Ver Sacrum *23, 1901 and is reproduced by courtesy of the Hunterian Art Gallery, University of Glasgow, Mackintosh Collection*

3.13 *Charles Rennie Mackintosh and*
Margaret Macdonald Mackintosh,
Music Room, House for an Art Lover,
1900, published in Meister der
Innenkunst, *Darmstadt 1902.*
Photograph courtesy of the Hunterian
Art Gallery, University of Glasgow,
Mackintosh Collection

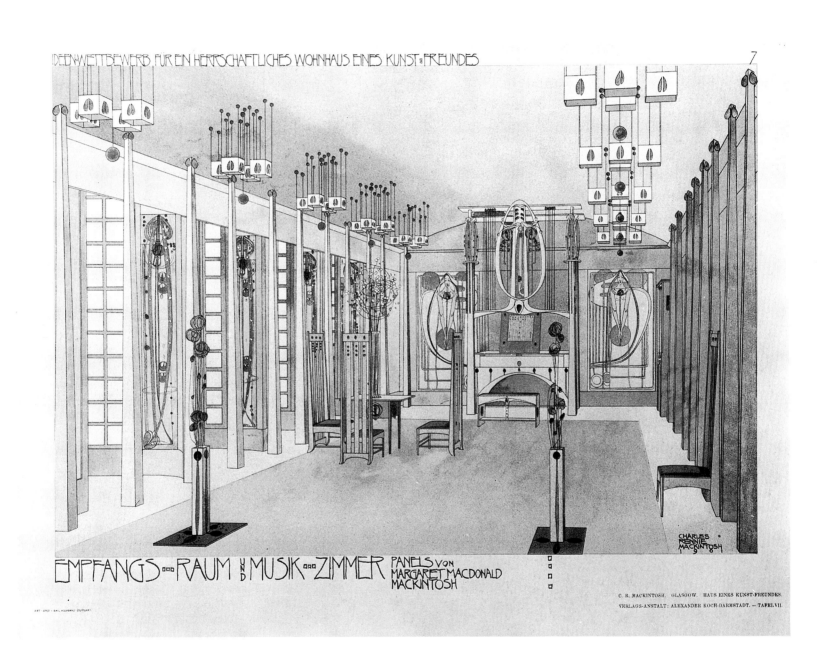

(cat. 84), and contrasted sharply with his more masculine ideas for Windyhill (1901).

As the Mackintoshes were to influence Viennese design, so in turn the sense of luxury Mackintosh achieved was influenced by Vienna. Later, around 1904 a new tension appeared in the furniture design of both Mackintosh and Hoffman, heralding an affinity between Glasgow and Vienna. That year Mackintosh's chair design was at its most continental: his ebonised chairs for Hill House (cat. 92) and bedroom chairs for Miss Cranston's house at Nitshill came closer to contemporary work by Hoffman than the work of any other British designer. The link between Arts and Crafts in Britain and Vienna had also consolidated with the founding in 1903 of the Wiener Werkstätte, the design and crafts studios which were to be 'an island of tranquillity' for Hoffmann amid the din of industrialisation. In setting up the Werkstätte its financial backer, Wärndorfer, had consulted Mackintosh, but though the Scottish designer did design a WW (Wiener Werkstätte) signet that was subsequently used in various media by the Werkstätte, his involvement was purely advisory.[40]

Following his success at the eighth Vienna Secession, Mackintosh entered a portfolio of designs in the *Haus eines Kunstfreundes* (House for an Art Lover) competition announced in the journal *Zeitschrift für Innendekoration* by its proprietor, the architect and publisher Alexander Koch (1860-1939) of Darmstadt. Koch shared Mackintosh's belief in the importance of individualism in design; he believed that good design showed 'intelligence, taste, unique ideas and the highest possible indigenous spirit'. Darmstadt was already on the Arts and Crafts map: at the request of the Grand Duke of Hesse (who had recently employed Baillie Scott and Ashbee's Guild), Olbrich had established an artists' colony there in 1899. The judges of the *Haus eines Kunstfreundes* competition (including Olbrich) disqualified Mackintosh's entry (*Der Vogel*, the bird) for an insufficient number of perspectives, but they commented on its 'distinctive colouring, impressive design and achievement of inner and outer construction' and gave him a purchase prize of 600 marks. No first prize was awarded. Like those of Baillie Scott, who won the second prize with a castellated folk-style entry, and Leopold Bauer of Vienna, who won the third, Koch published Mackintosh's design in 1902 as a *Meister der Innenkunst* portfolio. Margaret collaborated with her husband, and worked on the stencilling, embroidery and gesso designs for the music room, the drawing room and the nursery (fig 3.13). The difficulties surrounding the recent construction of the house in Bellahouston Park, Glasgow, is one indication of the precedence the couple gave artistic considerations over functional ones.

Continental publishers, manufacturers, artists and curators helped to publicise Glasgow art and design. Alexander Koch's broad interest in Glasgow design and the sheer number of his publishing enterprises set him apart. Besides initiating the *Haus eines Kunstfreundes* competition and the *Meister der Innenkunst* folios, Koch was also responsible for the catalogue of the Turin International Exhibition. His periodical *Moderne Stickereien* (1903-09) helped propagate the craft aspect of Glasgow design outside Scotland. But Koch's most influential journal must have been his *Deutsche Kunst und Dekoration*, which regularly featured commentaries on Glasgow design. He commissioned at least one cover design for the journal (May 1902) from Margaret Macdonald Mackintosh, and published many of her husband's designs for the *Dresdener Werkstätten für Handwerkskunst* in 1904, which probably ensured his inclusion among a small number of other architects invited to exhibit their work in Berlin in 1905.

The relationship between designers, patrons, publishers and critics in Glasgow and abroad, particularly in Austria and Germany,[41] was often one of friendship as much as business. Muthesius and his wife Anna were close to both the Newberys and Mackintoshes, and their son Eckhart considered himself fortunate to have had Newbery and Mackintosh as his godfathers.[42] But the Glasgow movement was developed by a wide range of professionals and its success depended just as much on the wholehearted dedication of men and women employed daily in the crafts or manufactures in the city as on the vision of the 'premier league', internationally oriented Newberys and Mackintoshes. Turn-of-the-century Glasgow design was something quite unique: straddling both the Arts and Crafts and Modernist movements, it embraced past values and innovation simultaneously, and its practitioners developed that 'sum of tradition' (to borrow Jessie Newbery's phrase) with immense intuition and panache. As Muthesius wrote in his introduction to the Mackintosh folio of *Meister der Innenkunst*:

[...] the Glasgow Style [...] has brought new values into the turmoil of the artistic manifestation of our time. It is independent to a high degree and bears the stamp of breeding and character. More than that it has a contagious effect. The stimulus it has given is felt not only in Glasgow, it has penetrated deep into the Continent and certainly as far as Vienna where it has found fertile soil.[43]

Footnotes

1. Hermann Muthesius, *Das englische Haus*, 1904: English edition, *The English House*, ed. with an intro. by Dennis Sharp, 1979 (repr. Oxford 1987), p. 51. Quoted by kind permission of BSP Professional Books, Oxford.

2. *Ibid.*, p. 54

3. Brian Blench *et al.*, *The Glasgow Style*, Glasgow 1984, pp. 9, 43.

4. Perilla Kinchin and Juliet Kinchin, *Glasgow's Great Exhibitions: 1888, 1901, 1911, 1938, 1988* (Wendlebury 1988), p. 21. Sellars chose the oriental style not for its 'suitability to the purpose, but because it lends itself readily to execution in wood'.

5. *Ibid.*

6. *Ibid.*, p. 23.

7. In Birmingham, for example, technical classes on materials were introduced. In the late 1880s the director of that city's School of Art, Edward R. Taylor, had started courses, such as repoussé metalwork, in which design was based on the handling of materials. Classes in 'designs executed in the materials for which they were intended', instituted by the academic year 1893-94, included enamelling, needlework, leatherwork, wood engraving, *sgraffito* and tempera: see Gleeson White, 'Some Glasgow Designers', *The Studio* 22 (1897), p. 48. Similar classes were offered by the 'Art Sheds' (Liverpool University's school of architecture and applied art) in the late 1890s. Each school assembled examples of indigenous and foreign crafts in small museum displays and students were encouraged to travel in order to witness foreign architecture and crafts. At the School of Applied Art in Edinburgh, which opened in 1892 under the direction of the architect Robert Rowand Anderson, the curriculum was dominated by the study of Scots architecture and historic, principally domestic, furnishings.

8. Quoted by White, *op. cit.* (note 7), p. 48.

9. These organisations included, for instance, the Scottish Industrial Art Association, 'set up by the exhibitors in the Artisans' and Women's Sections of the Scottish Exhibitions' of 1886 (Edinburgh) and 1888 (Glasgow) with branches throughout Scotland, and the Glasgow and West of Scotland Technical College (an amalgamation of four older colleges founded in 1884 and a forerunner of the University of Strathclyde).

10. Quoted by White, *op. cit.* (note 7), p. 48.

11. W.R. Lethaby, 'Art and Workmanship', in *The Imprint*, London 1913.

12. Newbery's contribution early in his Glasgow career to the 'Edinburgh Congress' (the 1889 Meeting of the National Association for the Advancement of Art and its Application to Industry) was a paper on 'The Place of Art Schools in the Economy of Applied Art' which emphasised his School's commitment to commerce and industry. But in this paper Newbery was also keen to emphasise that art and design schools could and should lead from the front line: schools existed to turn out designers rather than products, and to advance rather than follow public taste.

13. *The Studio* 24 (1901), p. 178.

14. *Glasgow Evening News*, 22 May 1895: quoted by Liz Bird in 'The Glasgow Style: Women and Art Education' in Jude Burkhauser (ed.), *Glasgow Girls: Women in Art and Design 1880-1920*, Edinburgh 1990, p. 72.

15. See Liz Arthur, 'Jessie Newbery (1864-1948)' in *Glasgow Girls*, *op. cit.* (note 14), p. 148.

16. White, *op. cit.* (note 7), p. 48.

17. See, for example, William Buchanan (ed.), *Mackintosh's Masterwork: The Glasgow School of Art*, Glasgow 1989.

18. *St Mungo*, 13 May 1897, p. 4: quoted by Perilla Kinchin in *Tea and Taste: The Glasgow Tea Room 1875-1975*, Wendlebury 1991, p. 89. St Mungo, or Kentigern, is the patron saint of Glasgow.

19. Quoted in *Tea and Taste*, *op. cit.* (note 18), p. 90.

20. E.W. Godwin, 'On some buildings I have designed', in *The British Architect* 10 (1878), p. 211: quoted in Pamela Robertson (ed.), *Charles Rennie Mackintosh. The Architectural Papers*, Wendlebury and Glasgow 1990, p. 23.

21. Quoted by permission of the Hunterian Art Gallery, University of Glasgow, Mackintosh Collection. According to Robert Macleod (and John Archer), the lecture was probably delivered to the Northern Art Workers' Guild on 6 January 1902: see *The Architectural Papers*, *op. cit.* (note 20), p. 213.

22. *The Architectural Papers*, *op. cit.* (note 20), pp. 204-05. Quoted by kind permission of the Hunterian Art Gallery, University of Glasgow, Mackintosh Collection.

23. Lecture delivered in 1893, entitled 'Architecture', now preserved in the Mackintosh Collection of the Hunterian Art Gallery. See *The Architectural Papers*, *op. cit.* (note 20), pp. 201-11.

24. *The English House*, *op. cit.* (note 1), p. 52: quoted by kind permission of BSP Professional Books, Oxford.

25. For a detailed history of Glasgow stained glass firms and designers in the late nineteenth century see Michael Donnelly, *Glasgow Stained Glass: A Preliminary Study*, 2nd ed., Glasgow 1985.

26. Widar Halén, *Christopher Dresser*, Oxford 1990, p. 203.

27. For discussions of various aspects of the eighteenth-century revival in furniture, architectural and garden design, see Stefan Muthesius, 'Why do we buy old furniture? Aspects of the authentic antique in Britain 1870-1910', in *Art History* 11.2 (June 1988), pp. 231-54, and Richard A. Fellows, *Reginald Blomfield*, London 1985.

28. For a history of the Wylie & Lochhead firm, see two articles by Juliet Kinchin, 'The Wylie & Lochhead Style' in the *Journal of the Decorative Arts Society* 9 (1985), pp. 4-16, and 'From the Cradle to the Grave: Wylie & Lochhead and the Furnishing of Death', in *Aspects of Scottish Decorative Art in the Twentieth Century*, Yearbook of the Scottish Society for Art History, 1988, pp. 4-10.

29. White, *op. cit.* (note 7), p. 48.

30. *Ibid.*

31. H. Jennings, *Our Homes and How to Beautify Them*, London 1902, p. 57: quoted in 'The Wylie & Lochhead Style' *op. cit.* (note 28), p. 7.

32. Juliet Kinchin, *op. cit.* (note 28), pp. 11, 16.

33. *Ibid.*

34. See Peter Vergo *et al.*, *Vienna 1900*, Edinburgh 1983, pp. 40-41.

35. Roger Billcliffe, *The Complete Furniture, Furniture Drawings and Interior Designs*, 3rd ed., London 1986, p. 54.

36. Ludwig Hevesi, *Acht Jahre Secession*, Vienna 1906, p. 288: quoted by Peter Vergo in *Art in Vienna 1898-1918*, Oxford 1981, p. 64.

37. For a discussion of the Beethoven frieze, see Peter Vergo, *Art in Vienna 1898-1918*, *op. cit.* (note 36), pp. 69-77, as well as Peter

Vergo, 'Gustav Klimt's Beethoven Frieze', in *The Burlington Magazine* 65 (1973), pp. 109-113.

38. A.S. Levetus, 'The Wiener Werkstätte', in *The Studio* 52 (1911), p. 187.

39. Ludwig Hevesi, *op. cit.* (note 36), p. 288.

40. Peter Vergo, *Art in Vienna 1898-1918, op. cit.* (note 36), p. 132.

41. See Jude Burkhauser, 'Artistic Dress Movement in Glasgow' in *Glasgow Girls, op. cit.* (note 14), p. 54: cultural links with Germany extended to Walter Blackie sending his children to school there and employing German domestic staff. Dennis Sharp discussed British-German cultural and economic relations in the late nineteenth century in his essay 'Mackintosh and Muthesius', in Patrick Nuttgens (ed.), *Mackintosh and his Contemporaries*, London 1988, pp. 8-17.

42. For a detailed account of the friendship between the Mackintoshes and the Muthesiuses, see Eckart Muthesius, 'Thoughts on my Godfather', in *Mackintosh's Masterwork, op. cit.* (note 17), pp. 9-10.

43. Hermann Muthesius, in the preface to the Mackintosh folio of *Meister der Innenkunst*, Darmstadt 1902, p. 3.

Biographical notes

Margaret De Courcy Lewthwaite Dewar
1878-1959

De Courcy (as she liked to be called) Lewthwaite Dewar was born in Ceylon (Sri Lanka), the daughter of a tea planter. She was educated both privately and at the High School for Girls in Glasgow. She received her art training at the Glasgow School of Art and the Central School of Arts and Crafts in London between 1892 and 1900. She was awarded the diploma of the Glasgow School of Art in 1914.

From 1902 until 1908, and again from 1912 until the 1920s, Dewar was Instructor in Enamels at the School of Art. A member of the Glasgow Society of Lady Artists from 1905, she won their Lauder award in 1935 for a zinc presentation casket with enamel plaques, and served as president of the Society 1934-37 and 1952-55. Dewar exhibited not only enamels and metalwork but also watercolours and oils internationally. Her work is characterised by strong colours and vigorous outlines.

John Ednie
1876-1934

The eldest son of a railway engineer, John Ednie was born in Glasgow but raised in Edinburgh, where, on leaving school, he enrolled at the Heriot Watt College. In 1897 he won a travel scholarship to study English architecture and interior decoration. After further travel in Europe he apprenticed himself to Scott Morton, an internationally respected Edinburgh firm of decorators, and to the architect John Kinross. Ednie was recruited by the Glasgow retailers and furnishers Wylie & Lochhead to work in their design department alongside George Logan. He won recognition as a designer for his dining room in the Wylie & Lochhead pavilion at the 1901 Glasgow International Exhibition, which was sent to Budapest the following year. He also exhibited in Turin in 1902. Possibly through the recommendation of his elder brother Andrew, a designer with the Edinburgh firm of Morrison & Co., John Ednie lectured on cabinet design at his old College in Edinburgh in 1903-06. Thereafter he worked full-time in Glasgow as director of the Industrial Art Section of the Glasgow and West of Scotland Technical College.

After leaving Wylie & Lochhead in 1906 Ednie began designing on a freelance basis. Besides private work he produced designs for various manufacturers, including the furniture firm Garvie & Sons of Aberdeen and the Glasgow stained-glass makers McCulloch & Co. In interior design his work included the

Margaret Gilmour
1860-1942

Jessie Marion King
1875-1949

remodelling of 26 Huntly Gardens and 'Dumbiedykes' in Whittinghame Drive, Glasgow. Together with John Taylor he wrote a book, *New Ideas for Home Decoration*, for the American market.

Ednie was one of a number of Arts and Crafts exponents in Glasgow who believed in the unity of art, craft and design. He was a member of the Scottish Guild of Handicraft and the Edinburgh Architectural Association, through which he maintained a number of professional links. In 1926, however, he moved to London with his wife Lily. Two years later they settled in Cairo, where Ednie accepted an appointment as director of the School of Art.

One of eleven children of John Gilmour, a muslin merchant, Margaret Gilmour was born in Glasgow and studied at Glasgow School of Art in 1877-1880. Together with her sister, Mary Ann Bell Gilmour (1872-1938), she established a studio at 179 West George Street in Glasgow, where both of them taught metalwork (particularly brass and pewter), embroidery, leatherwork, ceramic decoration, wood carving and staining, and painting. They produced a wide range of domestic items in beaten metal for the local market, though Margaret did have a stand of her own at the Glasgow International Exhibition of 1901. She and her sister regularly showed their work at exhibitions organised by the Glasgow Society of Lady Artists, and Margaret exhibited in Budapest in 1902. She died in Glasgow.

The daughter of the Rev. James W. King of Bearsden, near Glasgow, Jessie King attended the Glasgow School of Art in 1893 full-time. She had a talent for drawing and soon distinguished herself as one of the major figures of the new Glasgow movement with her distinctively rhythmic, linear style. Her individuality attracted the attention of *The Studio* which, by frequently publishing her work, helped establish her reputation. King soon embarked on a successful career as a book illustrator and was associated with over seventy titles, some of which she herself had compiled or written. From 1899 she taught the design and bookbinding course at Glasgow School of Art; in 1904 she took temporary charge of the Embroidery Department and, in 1907, taught design for the ceramic decoration course. During this time her versatility became apparent as she designed costumes for pageants, gesso panels, wallpapers, fabrics, posters and bookplates. She also produced interior designs and decorations. King designed silver, jewellery and fabrics, some of which were commissioned by (and others sold through) Liberty & Co. The fabrics were either woven by Alexander Morton & Co. or printed by Thomas Wardle, who had produced many of William Morris's designs. Her

George Logan
1866-1939

reputation was not confined to Scotland: she received a gold medal for her contribution to the 1902 Turin exhibition and exhibited in Cork, Berlin and Calcutta.

In 1908 Jessie King married E.A. Taylor, whose career took them first to Manchester and then in 1911 to Paris, where the couple ran a studio gallery for the fine and decorative arts. Forced home by the First World War, the Taylors settled in Greengate Close, Kirkcudbright. There Jessie developed her interests in batik and ceramic decoration; she became a prolific pottery painter and left much unfinished ware in her studio on her death. The Taylors kept a cottage on the island of Arran, where they taught sketching classes in the summer.

King exhibited widely but most often at Glasgow's Society of Lady Artists; she joined the Society in 1905 and won their Lauder award in 1921. Like many other women designers in Glasgow, she made her own very individual clothes. At the time of her death she was widely known and highly respected.

The creative partnership between George Logan, E.A. Taylor, John Ednie and the Glasgow furniture makers Wylie & Lochhead was central to the Glasgow Style. Of these designers, it was Logan who had the earliest and longest association with the company. He was born in Beith, a town about twenty miles southwest of Glasgow. After serving a traditional cabinetmaker's apprenticeship with one of the firms that had made the town a centre of furniture making in Scotland, he was invited to join Wylie & Lochhead in about 1882 - after, that is, the London firm of Waring and Gillow had unsuccessfully tried to tempt him south. Unlike many of his contemporaries, Logan remained in the Glasgow area for the rest of his life.

In 1901, Logan designed the library and bedroom of Wylie & Lochhead's pavilion at the Glasgow International Exhibition. The following year, the interior was chosen for exhibition at the British Arts and Crafts Exhibition in Budapest. On that occasion, Logan had both designed the pavilion and helped arrange the interiors. During the same year, he exhibited a screen in walnut with silver and semi-precious stones, together with an accompanying desk. The design, which incorporated a drawing by Jessie M. King, the future wife of E.A. Taylor, won Logan a silver medal. His professional relationship with Taylor continued in both their work for Wylie & Lochhead and in the Furniture Department

of the Glasgow and West of Scotland Technical College, which they ran between 1899 and the outbreak of the First World War. Logan continued to design for Wylie & Lochhead until about 1937, though he increasingly enjoyed painting. The titles of the works he exhibited at the Royal Glasgow Institute of Fine Arts - 'Aeolian Music', 'Song of Solomon' and 'Angels' - illustrate his interest in music and dedication to evangelism. He was a lay preacher and wrote poems and prayers for the *Greenock Telegraph*.

Ann Macbeth

1875-1948

Born in Bolton, Lancashire, the eldest of nine children of a Scottish engineer, Ann Macbeth enrolled in Glasgow School of Art in 1897. In 1899 she won a prize for needlework and in 1901 was appointed assistant instructress to Jessie Newbery. Her embroidery was highly regarded and regularly featured in *The Studio*. She exhibited at the Glasgow International Exhibition of 1901 and won a silver medal at Turin in 1902. In 1904 she took charge of the embroidery classes for teachers. She began teaching metalwork in 1906, bookbinding from 1907 and ceramic decoration from 1912. In 1908 she succeeded Jessie Newbery as head of the Embroidery Department of the School of Art and joined the staff council. In the course of the following three years she consolidated the work of the Department and lectured widely in Scotland and England on the teaching of needlework. This culminated in *Educational Needlework* (1911) which she co-authored with Margaret Swanson, an Ayrshire teacher who had devised a method of teaching children. This book was extremely influential and the Department attracted widespread attention as a result. The graduates were in much demand, and appointed to posts throughout Britain and abroad. Some of the advanced students also taught in schools, factories and the guild classes of the co-operative societies, besides organising needlework as employment for wounded soldiers during the First World War. In 1914 Ann Macbeth was invited by the Froebel

Union to draw up a programme of work for a diploma course in handiwork. Her interest in teaching needlework continued to grow: in 1918 she published *The Playwork Book*, in 1920 *Schools and Fireside Crafts* with Mary Spence, *Embroidered Lace and Leatherwork* in 1924, *Needleweaving* in 1926 and *The Countrywoman's Rug Book* in 1929.

Despite her teaching commitments, Macbeth continued to produce a great deal of her own work. In the beginning she was influenced by Jessie Newbery, whose views she shared, and though she made many practical items she also created purely decorative panels. She designed carpets for Alexander Morton & Co. as well, and fabrics for Donald Bros. of Dundee, Liberty & Co. and Knox's Linen Thread Company. Though Macbeth had lost her sight in one eye as a child she was a fine draughtswoman. She regarded the human figure as the embroiderer's ultimate challenge and from 1909 students produced a figure panel as their final piece of work. Her strong colour sense is also evinced by the wider range of colour she and her students used than in the early days of the Department.

In 1920 Macbeth moved to the Lake District but maintained her association with the Glasgow School of Art as a visiting instructress until her retirement in 1928. Throughout her career, Ann Macbeth's work was shown at national and international exhibitions. She received honorary diplomas from Paris, Tunis, Ghent, Budapest and Chicago. After retirement she continued to exhibit at the Glasgow Society of Lady Artists, who awarded the Lauder prize in 1930 and 1938.

Charles Rennie Mackintosh

1868-1928

Mackintosh was born in Glasgow, the son of a police superintendent. Apprenticed to the architect John Hutchison, he attended classes at the Glasgow School of Art. In 1889 he joined the practice of Honeyman & Keppie, where he met Herbert MacNair. At the School of Art he also met Margaret Macdonald (whom he was to marry in 1900) and her sister Frances. These four artists and architect-designers, whose work shared a symbolist identity, became a recognised group in the 1890s and were referred to as 'The Four'. They showed together at the Turin International Exhibition of Decorative Art in 1902.

At first Mackintosh designed architecture and furniture in accordance with the Arts and Crafts movement, but in the later 1890s his visual sensibilities developed dramatically. His work from this time not only showed an awareness of indigenous tradition and the organic principles of Arts and Crafts, but also began to embrace the positive values of Modernism. In the early 1900s his design became progressively less gothic (in the artistic and natural sense) and more fundamentally classical. In his mature work Mackintosh achieved a purity and intensity unsurpassed in British design.

In 1897 Mackintosh won the competition for a new building to house the Glasgow School of Art and received his first of many commissions from Catherine Cranston to design tea room interiors. In the decade 1895-1905 Mackintosh also executed a number of Glasgow public buildings, including Martyrs' Public School (1895), Queen's Cross Church (1897) and Scotland Street School (1904). Between 1900 and 1905 he exhibited (e.g. Vienna 1900, Turin 1902, Moscow 1903, Berlin 1905) and was published abroad. It was also during these years that he designed and, together with Margaret, furnished his most important houses, including Windyhill in Kilmacolm (1900) for William Davidson, and Hill House in Helensburgh (1902) for Walter Blackie. He designed the second phase of the School of Art in 1906, but not long thereafter the commissions came to a halt. In 1913 Mackintosh finally resigned from his firm, now Honeyman, Keppie & Mackintosh. The Mackintoshes decided to move south, first to Walberswick in 1914 and the following year to London where they settled in Chelsea. When war made the practice of architecture impossible, Mackintosh turned to textile

Margaret Macdonald Mackintosh
1864-1933

Frances Macdonald MacNair
1873-1921

design, producing avant-garde work that was either organic or geometric but above all vigorous and colourful.

Mackintosh's last major architectural commission (1915) was to remodel the Northampton home of W.J. Bassett-Lowke. In 1923 the Mackintoshes closed their house in Chelsea and moved to the south of France. There Mackintosh painted a number of watercolour landscapes with a brilliant clarity of structure and colour. In 1927 he returned to London, and died there of cancer the following year.

Margaret Macdonald was born in Tipton near Wolverhampton. With her family she moved to Glasgow in 1890, enrolling with her sister Frances in the School of Art. Having demonstrated her talent for a variety of art and craft media, including watercolour, embroidery and metalworking, she opened a professional studio with Frances at 128 Hope Street. At the School of Art she had met Charles Rennie Mackintosh, whom she married in 1900. Their collaborative interior and furniture designs were some of their finest work. Especially in the years 1900 to 1904, the couple blended Arts and Crafts, Aestheticism and Modernism.

In 1915 the Mackintoshes settled in Chelsea, London. In 1923-27 they lived in Collioure and Port Vendres in the south of France. After Charles died in London in 1928, Margaret returned briefly to France, but spent the last five years of her life alone in London. She produced almost nothing after 1922.

Between 1895 and 1924 Margaret contributed to more than forty exhibitions, including the Arts and Crafts Exhibition Society in London, the Vienna Secession and the Turin International Exhibition of Decorative Art. Her work was liberally illustrated and praised in a number of journals, including *The Studio* in Britain, *Dekorative Kunst* and *Deutsche Kunst und Dekoration* in Germany and *Ver Sacrum* in Austria. She served on the committee of the Royal Scottish Society of Painters in Watercolours (of which she had been elected a member in 1898) from 1907 until 1913.

Born in Kidsgrove, Frances was the youngest daughter of John Macdonald, a consulting engineer, and Frances Hardeman. The family moved to Glasgow in 1890. With her sister Margaret, Frances attended the School of Art, where she met James Herbert MacNair. By 1896 the Macdonald sisters had their own studio at 128 Hope Street, where they worked principally in watercolours and beaten metalwork. After marrying MacNair in 1899, Frances lived in Liverpool until 1905; there she taught embroidery at the 'Art Sheds', the School of Architecture and Applied Art run by University College, and assisted with the University tableaux. Returning to Glasgow in 1908, she was appointed Assistant Instructress in both the embroidery classes (run by Ann Macbeth) and the Saturday morning classes, and also assisted in design classes for metalwork and enamelwork until 1911. Frances MacNair offered a class at Liverpool on a visit in 1912. As she had worked closely with Margaret, so she collaborated with MacNair on the design of metalwork, jewellery and furniture. With Margaret and her husband Charles Rennie Mackintosh the MacNairs exhibited at the 1902 International Exhibition of Decorative Art in Turin where they presented a writing room. Relatively little of her work has survived since her husband destroyed much of it after her death.

James Herbert MacNair
1868-1955

Herbert MacNair was the son of a prosperous
Glasgow engineer. He was apprenticed to the
architect John Honeyman, in whose office he
met Charles Rennie Mackintosh. MacNair
studied part-time at the Glasgow School of Art
from c. 1888 until 1893-1894. In 1895,
MacNair left Honeyman & Keppie (as the firm
was named in 1889) and opened a design office
at 227 West George Street. There he specialised
in furniture, book illustration and plates,
posters and watercolours. Much of MacNair's
early work was lost in a studio fire in 1897.
MacNair and Mackintosh had met the
Macdonald sisters, Margaret and Frances, at
the School. By the mid-1890s 'The Four' were
close friends and associates. In 1899 Herbert
MacNair married Frances Macdonald. The
previous year he had moved to Liverpool to
teach at University College. In Liverpool
MacNair designed an interior for Professor
Davies, Dean of the Faculty of Arts at the
university, as well as his own house at 54
Oxford Street. He also designed metalwork
and jewellery, book covers, stage costumes,
tableaux and, in collaboration with C.J. Allen,
two university medals. In 1899 MacNair was
elected a member of the Liverpool Academy.
He exhibited internationally in Vienna in 1900
and Turin in 1902. After the closure of the 'Art
Sheds' at University College in 1905 he taught
drawing and painting, in association with
Gerald Chowne, at an independent studio at
Sandon Terrace, Liverpool. The collapse of the
family firm in 1908 brought the MacNairs
back to Glasgow. Herbert MacNair ceased to
paint or design after the tragic death of Frances
in 1921. They had a son, Sylvan, who became
executor of the Mackintosh estate on
Margaret's death in 1933.

Talwin Morris
1865-1911

Talwin Morris, the son of an auctioneer, was
born in Winchester and brought up by an
aunt. He was educated at Lancing College and
articled to an architect uncle, Joseph Morris, in
Reading. In 1891 he became the sub-Art
Editor of the journal *Black and White* in the
first year of its publication, which enabled him
to work in graphics. In 1893 Morris and his
wife Alice moved to Dunglass Castle, Bowling,
on his appointment as Art Director with the
publishers Blackie & Sons. As Art Director
Morris was responsible for all the graphics,
either in the text or on the bindings. Designs
were produced either by Morris and his small
staff or, increasingly, to commission.
Talwin Morris was never directly associated
with the Glasgow School of Art but he was a
friend of both Fra Newbery and Mackintosh;
in 1911 the latter was to design Morris's
tombstone. Morris introduced Mackintosh to
Walter Blackie who commissioned Hill
House. The work Morris executed for
Dunglass was featured in *The Studio* in 1897.
He exhibited repoussé metalwork - one of his
hobbies - in both Turin and Budapest in 1902.
He died unexpectedly in Bowling at the age of
forty-five.

Francis Henry Newbery
1853-1946

Francis Newbery was born in Membury,
Devon, the son of a shoemaker. In 1856 the
family moved to Bridport, Dorset, where
Francis attended the local School of Art. From
1875 he studied at the South Kensington
Schools, teaching at the same time at the
Cowper Street Corporation Schools and the
Grocers Company Schools in London. He
subsequently joined the staff of the Art
Training Schools at South Kensington to teach
drawing and painting.
In 1885 Newbery was appointed headmaster
of the Glasgow School of Art and Haldane
Academy where he revolutionised the teaching
of art and design. Believing in the equal
importance of craftwork and industrial design,
he established new classes for artisans and
craftworkers. 'Fra' Newbery especially
encouraged the training of women, appointing
many former students (including Jessie Rowat,
whom he had married in 1889) as teachers at
the School. Newbery also acted as a catalyst in
the careers of many designers, including 'The
Four' - Mackintosh, MacNair and the
Macdonalds. He took part in design activities
outside the city, serving on national and local
committees including the Edinburgh Social
Union, the Scottish capital's principal Arts and
Crafts organisation of the late 1880s and early
1890s.
The development of Glasgow design in the
1885-1920 period owed much to both the
Newberys. The importance of their active
encouragement of designers and architects at

Jessie Newbery
1864-1948

home and Fra Newbery's promotion of British, especially Glasgow, design abroad cannot be overemphasised. In 1902 Fra was responsible for the selection of Scottish design for the Turin International Exhibition of Decorative Art, for which he was awarded Italy's Order of the Crown.

On Fra's retirement in 1917, the couple moved to Corfe Castle in Dorset. Fra had been elected an artist member of the Glasgow Art Club in 1889 and was also a member of the Institute of Fine Art and Gravers. In Dorset he continued to paint, and presented a canvas - *The Romance of Bridport* - to the town, in recognition of which he was made a Freeman of the Borough. The Newberys had two daughters, Elsie and Mary, the latter herself a noted artist and designer and in the 1920s a member of the Edinburgh Group.

Born in Paisley, the daughter of a shawl manufacturer named William Rowat, Jessie Rowat attended schools there and in Edinburgh, and then continued her studies at Glasgow School of Art. She married the director of the School, Fra Newbery, in 1889. They had two daughters, Elsie and Mary. In 1894 Jessie Newbery organised embroidery classes, which became part of the School diploma course in applied design. The embroidery classes included Foliage in Outline, Study of Flowers from Nature, Design and Application and Technique and Study of Old Examples. The influence of John Ruskin and William Morris was obvious. By 1900 the Embroidery Department was well established and enjoyed widespread renown. In 1901 special classes were instituted for the training of teachers: this was a three-year course leading to a certificate of proficiency issued by the Scottish Education Department. The work of the Department was further recognised in 1907 when the School Governors were authorised to grant a Certificate of Art Needlework and Embroidery at the end of a two-year course. The Department was the only one in the school that awarded an individual certificate. Jessie Newbery also expressed her creativity and individuality in the clothes she made for herself. She embroidered collars, belts, yokes and cuffs which incorporated distinctive Russian metal clasps. Her style was adopted

by many of her students. She retired from teaching in 1908. During her years as head of the Embroidery Department her work was shown at exhibitions in Britain, France, Germany, Italy and the United States. Her work was also illustrated in many of the European art magazines of the period, notably *The Studio, Das Eigenkleid der Frau* and *Moderne Stickereien*. Though best remembered as an enthusiastic teacher and for her embroidery, she was also interested in other forms of art. In 1890 she was awarded a bronze medal for a stained-glass design entitled *Tempestas*. At the Arts and Crafts Exhibition Society in 1893 she exhibited an altar frontal, repoussé alms plate and chalice, all executed in Glasgow by Kellock Brown. In Turin in 1902 her work was represented by an embroidered bedspread and an Axminster carpet designed for Alexander Morton & Co. Jessie Newbery retired with her husband to Corfe Castle, Dorset.

Ernest Archibald Taylor
1874-1951

Born in Greenock, E.A. Taylor was the fifteenth of seventeen children. After school he trained as a draughtsman with the Clyde shipyard, Scott & Co. Ltd. From 1893 or 1894 he worked as a trainee designer with Wylie & Lochhead, during which time he attended Glasgow School of Art part-time and the furniture design classes run by the Glasgow and West of Scotland Technical College. Between 1900 and 1906 he taught furniture design for the College's Industrial Arts Department and was an Instructor and Lecturer in Furniture at the School of Art in 1903-1905.

Thanks to his success with the drawingroom of the Wylie & Lochhead pavilion at the 1901 Glasgow International Exhibition (which was transferred to Budapest in 1902), Taylor received two important commissions, to furnish 32 Radnor Road, Handsworth in Birmingham, and to design the interior of Douglas House, Pollokshields, Glasgow for the industrialist William Weir (later Lord Weir of Cathcart). At Budapest in 1902 Taylor exhibited stained-glass designs, a flower stand, a table and his designs for the Weir house. About 1906 he left Wylie & Lochhead and virtually abandoned interior design. Taylor was designer-manager for George Wragge & Co. of Manchester in 1907-11, for whom he

designed over one hundred stained-glass windows. In 1911 he moved to Paris with his wife, Jessie M. King, whom he had married in 1908. In the French capital he ran a small decorating studio, the 'Sheiling Atelier', and mixed socially with a circle of international artists including the Scots painters John Duncan Fergusson and Samuel John Peploe. In 1912 Taylor designed a series of stained-glass panels (unfortunately destroyed in the First World War) for the Aubervillier house of the industrialist M. Lazare Weiller. Taylor returned to Scotland in 1916 or 1917, after serving with the French Red Cross.

For E.A. Taylor, as for Jessie M. King, there was no division between the fine and the decorative arts; indeed, though he worked for most of his life as a designer, he regarded himself as an artist. In retirement he devoted himself to watercolour painting and exhibited regularly in Glasgow and Edinburgh.

George Henry Walton
1867-1933

George Walton was born in Glasgow. His father was Jackson Walton, an inventor of engineering components as well as a gifted amateur artist. Of George's eleven siblings, five pursued artistic careers, but it was George, the youngest, who combined his father's mechanical and artistic talents best. In 1888, when he was only twenty-one and had little formal training, George opened a decorating business in Glasgow's Wellington Street. His family's contacts - particularly those of his brother, the artist E.A. Walton - proved to be a rich source of commissions. After nearly a decade of continuous expansion, the firm became a limited company in 1896 with Walton as its director. George left the following year to pursue his career in London, while the firm continued to grow. In the wake of a commission to decorate tea rooms in Scarborough they opened an office in York in 1898. Walton's arrival in London built on this success: he was invited to decorate the Salon photographic exhibition at the Dudley Galleries in 1897; later the same year he repeated the process for the Eastman (Kodak) Photographic Exhibition at the New Galleries. Organised by a recently appointed assistant manager, George Davison, the Eastman Exhibition was not only a great success, but also the first of a series of substantial commercial and private commissions from Davison that continued for the next thirty

Hannah Moore Walton
1863-1940

Helen Walton
1850-1921

years. Between 1898 and 1903 Walton designed, decorated and furnished new Kodak showrooms in London (five branches), Glasgow, Dublin, Milan, Brussels, Vienna and Moscow. He also designed promotional and packaging material for Kodak and the wider photographic industry. In 1901 he received his first architectural commission for a private house at Elstree, Hertfordshire. This was followed later in the decade by two large houses for Davison: The White House, Shiplake, Oxfordshire and Wern Fawr, Harlech in Wales. Major interior schemes were also completed at The Philippines, Brasted, Kent, Alma House, Cheltenham and Finnart House, Weybridge, Surrey. Between 1916 and 1921 Walton was employed by the Central Liquor Traffic Control Board, for whom he redesigned public houses and canteens in the Carlisle area for the most part.

Though Walton's output declined after the War, he still carried out a wide variety of commissions. He devoted much time and energy to designing textiles for Morton Sundour Fabrics, though relatively few were actually produced. Fittingly, his last major work, completed in 1932, was a chapel in memory of George Davison at Antibes in southern France.

Hannah Walton was born in Glasgow. A skilled miniaturist, she also painted glass and china, and exhibited - like her elder sister Helen - in the 1888 Glasgow International Exhibition. From her home she taught painting and craft with her sister during the 1890s. An affiliated member of the Glasgow Society of Lady Artists, she exhibited regularly from 1896.

Helen Walton was born in Cardross and attended the Glasgow School of Art in about 1871. Between 1893 and 1904 she taught ceramic design and decoration at the School, having exhibited at the 1888 Glasgow International Exhibition. Her work was much in demand, especially for wedding presents. She taught from her home during the 1890s and, from 1893, was an honorary member of the Glasgow Society of Lady Artists.

Marion Henderson Wilson
1869-1956

Ellison J.F. Young
1886-1949

Marion Wilson was born in Glasgow. From 1884 until 1896 she attended the Glasgow School of Art. She was commended once and won two prizes in national and local competitions. Encouraged like most students to try a variety of disciplines, she showed an early preference for art metalwork which continued throughout her long and prolific career. Marion Wilson worked mainly in brass, copper and tin, combining fine craftsmanship and sensitive designs with a typical Glasgow Style repertoire - attentuated parallel forms, stylised hearts and cabbage roses - and Celtic motifs. From 1894 Wilson was a member of the Glasgow Society of Lady Artists.

Born in Glasgow, Ellison Young attended Hamilton Academy where she won a silver medal for Eminence in Art. She attended the evening classes at Glasgow School of Art and in 1907 won a prize for Excellence in Design. The following session she was awarded a free studentship and won the Messrs William Meikle & Sons Prize for Stained Glass. In 1908 she earned the Certificate for Art Needlework with the grade of Excellent. From 1909 until 1911 she was Assistant Governess of Westbourne School, Glasgow. She then attended the Glasgow & West of Scotland College of Domestic Science and gained a diploma in Dressmaking, Needlework and Millinery in 1913. She taught for a short while at Queens Park School, Glasgow and at Clydebank School. In 1914 she married the architect James Steel Maitland and, like all women teachers, was forced to retire on marriage. She lived in Paisley until her death in 1949.

May Craig

Vase
1914
height 7.8 cm; diameter 8.6 cm
signed and dated with printed
Rosenthal factory mark

Glasgow Museums and Art Galleries
E1987.36

This cylindrical vase, with its
slightly spread foot and everted
rim of Rosenthal porcelain, is
enamelled with four arched
panels, each of which contains a
female figure wearing
contemporary dress and holding
a document. Above the arcade
formed by the panels are flowers
reserved in white against a green
ground. The band below the
figures is inscribed with the text
of the *Te Deum:* 'WE PRAISE
THEE O GOD WE
ACKNOWLEDGE THEE TO
BE THE LORD'. Above the
shoulders of the figures the word
'ALLELUIA' is spelled out.
Little is known about May Craig.
On the evidence of this vase she
worked in the decorative Pre-
Raphaelite style of the later Arts
and Crafts movement. Her style
of art decoration, with its
combination of delicate figural
detailing and lettering, was
influenced by the graphic work
of Jessie M. King, who also
decorated blanks.

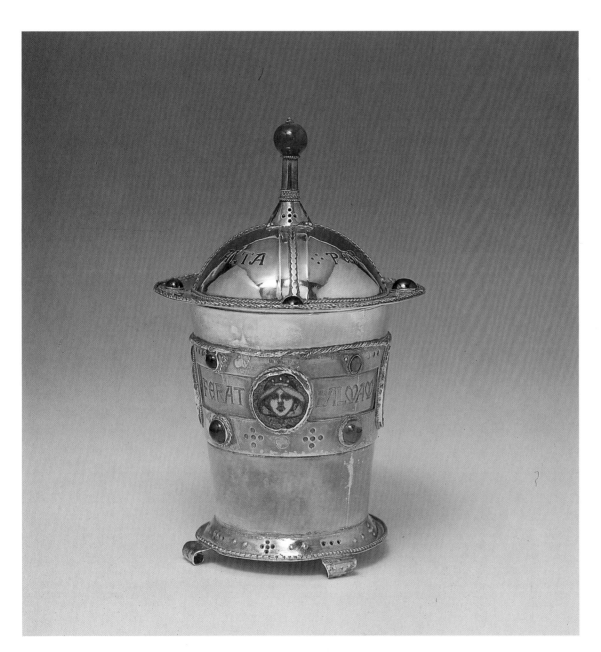

68
**Margaret De Courcy
Lewthwaite Dewar**

Cup and cover
1913
silver, set with enamel plaques,
cabochon stones and glass
height 18.2 cm
inscribed and dated on rim

*Glasgow Museums and Art Galleries
E1984.70*

The straight-sided conical body is
supported by a short skirt base
that rests on two cross stretchers,
the ends of which curl
downwards to form four feet. It
is decorated with a wide, applied
band round the centre with
ropework decoration and four
panels of enamel, two of which
bear female heads, the other
foliage. Between the enamels are
rectangular panels bearing the
inscription in Celtic script
'PALMAM QUI MERUIT,
FERA' ('Let him who has won
bear the palm', from John Jortin,
Lusus Poetici [1722], which
Admiral Lord Nelson later
adopted as a motto). Above and
below the inscription are
cabochon gemstones. The domed
cover has a flat overhanging rim
with a decorative, ropework
band, inset with four cabochon
gemstones; the rim is divided into
four sections by vertical
ropework and bears another
inscription in Celtic lettering,
'PER ARDUA AD ALTA'
('Through hardship the heights').
The cover is surmounted by a
cylindrical column topped by an
orange glass bead finial.
The original sketch for the cup
survives in a private collection.
The cup may have been designed
for use as a ciborium.

Exhibitions
1984   Glasgow
1990   Glasgow

Literature
Gerald and Celia Larner, *The Glasgow
Style,* Edinburgh 1979 (illus. 50).
Burkhauser, *Glasgow Girls* (illus. p. 158,
fig. 206).

69
John Ednie

Design for Ingleneuk
1902
pencil and colour wash on paper
29.6 x 37 cm

Glasgow Museums and Art Galleries
E1982.77.4

In 1909 John Wylie of the Glasgow furniture firm Wylie & Lochhead submitted a planning application for alterations to 26 Huntly Gardens, Glasgow. The plans and elevations included designs for a Billiard Room, Library, Cloakroom and Bathroom. This elevation, showing a large central fireplace and overmantel flanked by built-in seating, was the work of John Ednie. It closely relates to a detailed perspective for a 'New Billiards Room, Kelvinside, Glasgow' that he had exhibited at the Royal Scottish Academy. By contrast, the loose colouring, the alterations and the addition of dimensions to this design suggest that it was a working drawing for the actual scheme.

Collections
E.A. Taylor; Cecile MacLauchlan; with Sotheby's, Belgravia 1982

Exhibitions
1983   *Glasgow Style Designers,*
        Glasgow Museums and Art
        Galleries

Literature
Academy Architecture, London 1903, p. 61 (an illustration of the perspective previously exhibited at the RSA.)

Margaret Gilmour

Alms Dish
c. 1900
brass with enamel inlay
height 3.3 cm; diameter 58 cm

Glasgow Museums and Art Galleries
E1986.25

This large dish with shallow well
and raised central boss may have
been designed for church use or
simply as a tour-de-force
domestic piece. The wide rim is
decorated with a Celtic-inspired
motif of interlaced tails with
circles dramatically emphasised
by blue-green enamel inserts. The
same rim bears the monogram
MG.

Exhibitions
1901   Glasgow International
        Exhibition
1990   Glasgow

Literature
Burkhauser, *Glasgow Girls*, p. 166 (illus.
fig. 217).

71

Jessie M. King (designer)

*Menu Cover for Miss Cranston's
Lunch and Tea Rooms*
1917
26 x 8.9 cm (folded)

*Glasgow Museums and Art Galleries
PP1979.139*

Jessie M. King executed a wide
range of graphic designs, from
book illustrations and covers to
such items as this. Her work is
characterised by clear execution
and child-like vision. This
shepherdess watching over her
lambs emanates the gentle poetics
that distinguished her output,
enriched by her understated
technical brilliance. The card was
produced near the end of Miss
Cranston's domination of the
Glasgow tea-room scene. Four
locations are still listed on the
front, but by the end of the year
the ones in Argyle Street and
Buchanan Street had been sold.
Miss Cranston herself retired in
1919.

Literature
Burkhauser, *Glasgow Girls,* p. 37 (illus.
fig. 27).

72
Jessie M. King (designer)

Pendant
1900s
silver with green and blue enamel
in a stylised flower design with a
pearl drop
7 x 1.8 cm
Designed for Liberty &
Company

Glasgow Museums and Art Galleries
E1982.137.2

Collections
Irina Laski

Exhibitions
1984   Glasgow (70)
1990   Glasgow (124)

Literature
Gerald and Celia Larner, *The Glasgow
Style,* Edinburgh 1979 (illus. 202).

73
Jessie M. King (designer)

Pendant
1900s
silver with green and blue enamel
in a stylised flower design
28 cm (incl. chain, 9 cm excl.
chain) x 6.5 cm

Glasgow Museums and Art Galleries
E1982.137.4

Collections
Irina Laski

Exhibitions
1984   Glasgow (70)
1990   Glasgow (124)

Literature
Gerald and Celia Larner, *The Glasgow
Style,* Edinburgh 1979 (illus. 201).

74
Jessie M. King (designer)

Waist buckle
1906
two circles of silver with green,
blue, white and brown enamel,
worked in a design of stylised
birds and flowers
4 cm x 8.8 cm
hallmarked Liberty & Co. 1906
Designed for Liberty &
Company

Glasgow Museums and Art Galleries
E1982.137.7a and b

Collections
Irina Laski

Exhibitions
1984   Glasgow (69)
1990   Glasgow

Literature
Gerald & Celia Larner, *The Glasgow
Style*, Edinburgh 1979 (illus. 197).
Burkhauser, *Glasgow Girls* (p. 181, illus.
fig. 248).

75
Jessie M. King (designer)

Hand mirror
1906
silver with enamelled floral
decoration
28 x 12.7 cm
hallmarked Liberty & Co. 1906;
Rd. no. 479297
Designed for Liberty &
Company

Glasgow Museums and Art Galleries
E1982.164

Exhibitions
1984   Glasgow (71)

76

Jessie M. King (designer)

Waist buckle
1907
silver with green and blue enamel
in a design of stylised flowers and
birds
5.5 x 7.5 cm
hallmarked Liberty & Co.
Birmingham 1907

Glasgow Museums and Art Galleries
E1982.137.5a & b

Originally designed for Liberty
& Company, the buckle has since
been adapted for use as a brooch.

Collections
Irina Laski

Exhibitions
1984   Glasgow (69)
1990   Glasgow (119)

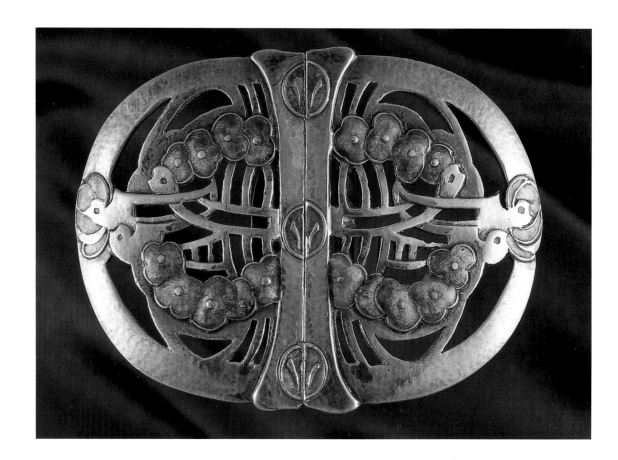

77

Jessie M. King (designer)

Waist buckle
1908
silver with green, blue and brown
enamel in a design of stylised
flowers and birds
5.5 x 6 cm
hallmarked Liberty & Co.
Birmingham 1908
Designed for Liberty &
Company

Glasgow Museums and Art Galleries
E1982.137.6a & b

Collections
Irina Laski

Exhibitions
1984   Glasgow (59)
1990   Glasgow (119)

Literature
Gerald and Celia Larner, *The Glasgow*
Style, Edinburgh 1979 (illus. 198)

78
George Logan

Design for the 'White Boudoir'
c. 1901
watercolour and pencil on
canvas, sewn with beads
67.5 x 76 cm (framed)

Glasgow Museums and Art Galleries
E1983.12.2

The design does not relate to any
known interior and is an
unfettered evocation of the
Glasgow Style rather than a
conventional design drawing for
a proposed scheme. The details of
the panelling and the beads sewn
to the canvas are indicative of
Logan's penchant for enriching
surfaces, as exemplified by his
design for a folding screen for the
Turin Exhibition of 1902 (cat.
79). The artist was keenly
interested in music and indeed his
graphic oeuvre often incorporates
musical themes. His two
daughters, who shared this
interest, probably served as
models for the girls playing the
piano in the background.

Collections
Miss Maxwell Russell, a great-niece of the
artist

Exhibitions
1902   Turin
1904   GIFA

1983   Turin
1983   *Glasgow Style Designers,*
        Glasgow Museums and Art
        Galleries
1984   Glasgow (72)

Literature
Academy Architecture, 1904.
The Studio, November 1905, p. 119.

79
George Logan (designer)

Folding screen
1901
walnut veneer, decorated with
silver, mother-of-pearl,
turquoise, red amethyst and an
unidentified white stone, the
central panel set with an ink and
watercolour drawing by Jessie M.
King
172.1 x 137.2 cm.

Glasgow Museums and Art Galleries
E.1896.52

Folding screens were popular
with Glasgow Style designers.
Taylor, Walton, MacNair and
Mackintosh all produced
examples of them. None
surpassed George Logan's three-
fold screen for the Scottish
section of the Turin International
Exhibition of 1902. The screen
was made by Wylie & Lochhead

and accompanied by a desk also
designed by Logan. The central
panel contains an ink and
watercolour drawing by Jessie M.
King entitled *Princesses of the
Red Rose.* The screen owes its
success to the balance between its
formal simplicity and its subtly
enriched surface. Logan
maintained the standard
rectangular shape, but pierced the
two side panels with an oval and
added a pointed detail to the top
and bottom. The stylised silver
rose motifs and the teardrops
running down the panels are
linked by shallow mouldings.
The detailing has the same
delicate, linear quality as Jessie
M. King's drawing.

Collections
Walter S. Strang, a Scotsman who had
emigrated to Australia in the 1890s;
screen and desk were both in Australia
between 1906 and 1929, when they were
brought back to Scotland on his
daughter's marriage; in 1937 the desk was
destroyed in a fire at her home.

Exhibitions
1902   Turin
1984   *The Folding Image,* Washington
        and New Haven
1990   *Scotland creates: 5000 years of
        art and design,* McLellan
        Galleries, Glasgow (G 21)

Literature
Deutsche Kunst und Dekoration 12 (Sept.
1902), p. 575 (detail illus.).
Dekorative Kunst 5 (August 1902), p.
402.
Gerald & Celia Larner, *The Glasgow
Style,* Edinburgh 1979, pl. 69.
M. Komanecky, 'The Restoration of
George Logan's "Rose Screen"', *The
Journal of the Decorative Arts Society* 9
(1985), pp. 17 - 22.
Roger Billcliffe, 'How many Swallows
make a Summer? Art and Design in
Glasgow in 1900', *Scotland Creates: 5000
Years of Art and Design,* London 1990, p.
148 (illus. 9.17).

80
Ann Macbeth

The Sleeping Beauty
1899-1900
beige silk with silk appliqué in cream, pink and fawn, embroidered with gold metal threads and silk threads of blue, pink, green, mauve, cream and black, using satin, stem and knot stitches with French knots and couching; one of the feet and the hair are padded
48.5 x 106.8 cm

Glasgow Museums and Art Galleries
E1989.9

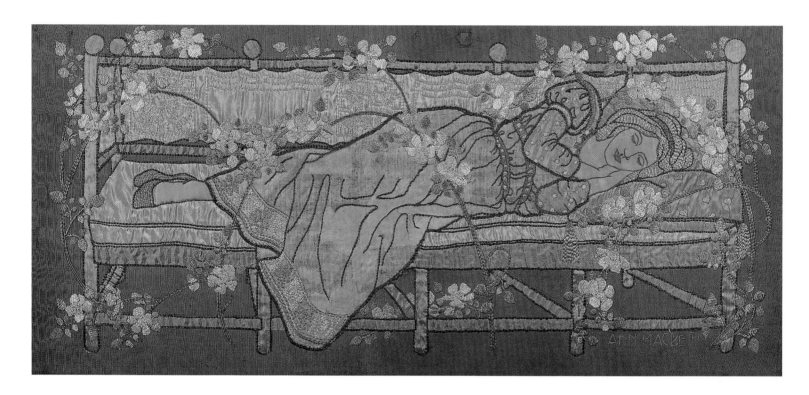

Designed and worked by Macbeth while she was a student of Jessie Newbery. A pen and ink drawing of similar design with colour was published in *The Studio* in 1902.

Collections
William McLean

Exhibitions
1902   Turin
1979   *Glasgow 1900,* The Fine Art Society, Glasgow
1980   Glasgow (35)
1990   Glasgow (294)

Literature
The Studio 29 (1903), p. 213.
Gerald and Celia Larner, *The Glasgow Style,* Edinburgh 1979 (illus. 142).
Liz Arthur, 'Glasgow School of Art Embroidery, 1894-1920', *The Journal of the Decorative Arts Society 1890-1940* 4, pp. 18 - 25.
Burkhauser, *Glasgow Girls,* p. 157 (illus. fig. 205).

81
Frances Macdonald

Mirror
c. 1896
beaten tin on wooden frame
73 x 73.6 cm

Glasgow Museums and Art Galleries
46.5a

The decoration of the border of the mirror combines two motifs that are particularly characteristic of early Glasgow Style: stylised, elongated human forms and forms of plants. In this example, female figures support the mirror surface and echo the stems and branches of the plant. The plant in this case is Honesty, the popular name for various varieties of *hunaria* (usually *hunaria biennis*), which have a cruciform purple or white flower and flat round semi-transparent seed pods (whence the name derives). Popular at the time, the pods are still used in flower arrangements.

Collections
Talwin Morris; Mrs Alice Talwin Morris; presented by her in 1939

Exhibitions
1933   *Mackintosh Memorial Exhibition* (116, as by Margaret and Frances Macdonald)
1952   *Victorian & Edwardian Decorative Arts,* Victoria & Albert Museum, London (R21)
1953   *Works by Charles Rennie Mackintosh,* Saltire Society and ACGB, Edinburgh (B16)
1960-61 *Sources of the Twentieth Century,* Musée National d'Art Moderne, Paris (42)
1968   *Charles Rennie Mackintosh: Architecture, Design and Painting,* Edinburgh and tour (181)
1982   *Charles Rennie Mackintosh,* Kunstindustrimuseum, Copenhagen
1983   Turin
1983-84 Margaret Macdonald Mackintosh, Hunterian Art Gallery, Glasgow (d)
1984   Glasgow (88)
1990   Glasgow

Literature
The Studio 11 (1897), p. 87 (illus.).
Nikolaus Pevsner, *The Sources of Modern Architecture and Design,* London 1968, p. 131 (illus.).
B. Coti, *L'Art du XIXe Siècle,* vol. 2, Editions Citadelles, Paris, fig. 416.
Gerald and Celia Larner, *The Glasgow Style,* Edinburgh 1979 (illus. 178).
Anthea Callen, *Angel in the Studio,* London 1979, pp. 150 - 151.

82 a, b
Frances Macdonald

Pair of Candlesticks
c. 1896
beaten brass
height 49.5 cm

Glasgow Museums and Art Galleries
46.5d

These monumental candlesticks, with curved strip handles, are also decorated with stylised floral motifs (see previous entry). The stems bear single roses, the bases a formalised, almost abstract, floral pattern with a central rose motif.

Collections
Talwin Morris; Mrs Alice Talwin Morris; presented by her in 1939

Exhibitions
1984   Glasgow (91)

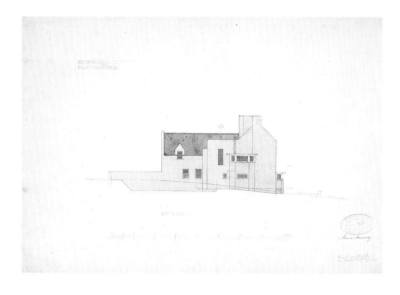

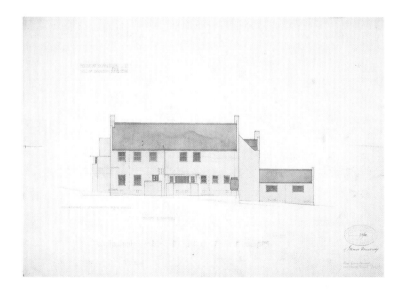

83
Charles Rennie Mackintosh

Designs for Windyhill,
Kilmacolm
1900

(a) north elevation
pencil and wash on paper
38.6 x 56 cm
signed

(b) east elevation
pencil and wash on paper
39.2 x 56.4 cm
signed

(c) west elevation
pencil and wash on paper
38.6 x 56 cm
signed

Hunterian Art Gallery (Mackintosh
Collection), University of Glasgow

Windyhill, in Kilmacolm,
Renfrewshire, was commissioned
around 1900 by William
Davidson Junior, son of William
Davidson of Gladsmuir,
Kilmacolm, himself a patron of
the architect. Davidson Jr.
already owned several pieces of
his furniture and in 1901
commissioned more of it for the
house: some of these simple,
natural oak pieces were among
the last of Mackintosh's pure
Arts and Crafts designs, whereas
other pieces were painted white.
The house was also typically Arts
and Crafts in many respects: it
referred not only to Scots
vernacular design and materials
but also to English design of the
late 1890s. The harled stone
walls, the long, low slate roofs,
the flat, wide 'west' chimney, the
casement windows and even the
green water butt all recall the
drawings of C.F.A. Voysey.
The exhibited drawings are three
of the nine stamped 7 August
1900 that were submitted for
planning permission to Renfrew
Dean of Guild. The final
(presumably second) set of plans
approved the following day are
now with Strathclyde Regional
Council. The amendments to the

drawings suggest that
Mackintosh had difficulty
orientating elevations: the
northern elevation was originally
labelled 'West', the eastern
'North' and the western 'South'.
The original floor plans (not
shown) are coloured olive green,
rose, dark blue and sepia -
colours often used by
Mackintosh in his designs for
furniture and decorations. The
principal change between them
and the later set of plans, which
were actually carried out, is the
first-floor bathroom added to the
south of the house.

Collections
Honeyman & Keppie; Ronald Harrison;
University of Glasgow

Exhibitions
1991   *Saved for Scotland*, National
        Gallery of Scotland, Edinburgh

Literature ('c' only)
National Art-Collections Fund Review,
London 1989, p. 201.
C.R. Mackintosh Architectural Drawings,
Glasgow 1990, p. 15 (illus. p. 20).

84

Charles Rennie Mackintosh

*Design for two cabinets for
Mrs Rowat*
1902
pencil and watercolour on paper
29.4 x 45.1 cm
inscribed and dated lower right
'140 Bath Street/ Glasgow 1902';
inscribed lower left *'Sketch
of/cabinet for/Mrs Rowat/14
Kingsbor/ough Gardens'*,
and upper right *'Silver doors/
inlaid with/coloured glass'*;
various other notes
scale 1:12

*Hunterian Art Gallery (Mackintosh
Collection), University of Glasgow
Mg)12*

Four cabinets were made
according to the exhibited design,
except for the chequered pattern
(to be inlaid or painted) on the
back panel of the cupboard
which was never carried out.
Two of them were built for Mrs
Rowat (Jessie Newbery's mother)
in 1902, the other two for the
Mackintoshes' own flat at 120
Main Street in Glasgow. The
latter pair is now in the studio-
drawingroom of the
reconstructed Mackintosh flat in
the Hunterian Art Gallery,
University of Glasgow. The two
pairs differ only with respect to
the metal door hinges: one pair
has two and the other four. The
cabinets were meant to be
painted white; their doors were
to be painted silver, set with
coloured glass inlays and kept
open (as they are in the exhibited
drawing). They are among the
most exquisite examples of
Mackintosh's furniture from the
period 1900-03. Each of the white
figures on the doors holds a pink
rose, a Glasgow Style motif used
liberally not only by the
Mackintoshes (see, for example,
cat. 37) but also by Jessie
Newbery and others associated
with the School of Art.

Collections
Mackintosh Estate, University of
Glasgow

Exhibitions
1985   *Mackintosh Cabinets*,
        Mackintosh House, Hunterian
        Art Gallery, Glasgow
1988-89 *Mackintosh Cabinets*,
        Mackintosh House, Hunterian
        Art Gallery, Glasgow
1991-92 *Charles Rennie Mackintosh
        Drawings*, Designs and
        Watercolours, Hunterian Art
        Gallery, Glasgow

Literature
Billcliffe, *Mackintosh Furniture and
Interiors*, p. 118 (D.1902.4).
*Charles Rennie Mackintosh at the
Hunterian Art Gallery*, University of
Glasgow, Glasgow 1991
(illus. p. 22).

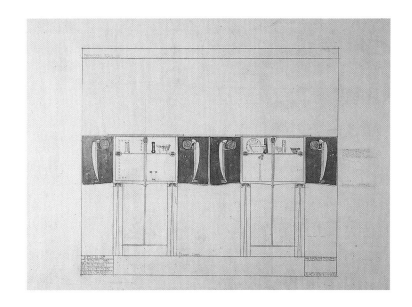

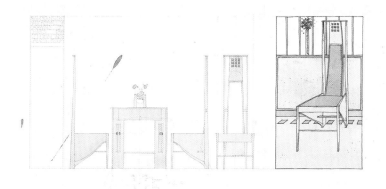

85
Charles Rennie Mackintosh

*Design for tables and chair with
high back for the Room de Luxe,
Willow Tea Rooms*
1903
pencil and watercolour on paper
32.8 x 51.4 cm
inscribed upper left *'Miss
Cranstons/Sauciehall St./drawing
for chairs for/central table/ladies
room'*, bottom *'2'5" high/4 like
this/3-3'6" circular/Greenock
Cabinet Co.'*, and right *'Leather
seat & back'*. Scale 1:12

*Hunterian Art Gallery (Mackintosh
Collection), University of Glasgow Nd)2*

The furniture was executed in
accordance with the exhibited
design.

Collections
Sylvan MacNair

Literature
Billcliffe, *Mackintosh Furniture and
Interiors*, p. 135 (D.1903.22).
Alan Piper, *Drawing for 3-Dimensional
Design*, London 1990 (illus.).

86
Charles Rennie Mackintosh

Textile design: tulip and lattice
c. 1915-23
watercolour and pencil on paper
39.7 x 28.8 cm

signed lower right '*Charles R. Mackintosh/2 Hans Studios/43a Glebe Place Chelsea*' and '*10 Inches*'

Hunterian Art Gallery (Mackintosh Collection), University of Glasgow Ic)17

Between 1915 and 1923 Mackintosh was living in London. In the absence of architectural commissions, he turned to designing textiles to help eke out a living. The companies he designed for included Liberty's, Templetons, F.W. Grafton and Co. of Manchester and William Foxton, a London manufacturer whose firm produced some of the most interesting textiles of the post-war period. Unfortunately, though Mackintosh is known to have designed for roller or block printed furniture and curtain fabric (as well as handkerchiefs), only two samples of fabric (now with the Victoria & Albert Museum, London) survive that can be positively identified as designed by him.

Over one hundred of Mackintosh's textile designs have survived. On the whole, they are either organic or geometric. This particular example is one of the most finished. Its combination of a severe lattice pattern with floral forms on the one hand, and of cool indigo with hot pink and orange on the other, make it also one of the most powerful.

Collections
William Davidson; Davidson Bequest; University of Glasgow

Exhibitions
n.d.   *British Sources of the Art Nouveau,* Whitworth Art Gallery, Manchester
1977   *Charles Rennie Mackintosh Flower Drawings,* London and tour (29)
1978   *The Chelsea Years,* Hunterian Art Gallery, Glasgow (1)
1982-83 *Charles Rennie Mackintosh Textiles,* Hunterian Art Gallery, Glasgow
1991-92 *Charles Rennie Mackintosh Drawings,* Designs and Watercolours, Hunterian Art Gallery, Glasgow

Literature
Billcliffe, *Mackintosh Textiles,* p. 36 (illus.).
Charles Rennie Mackintosh, Seibu Museum, Tokyo 1979 (illus. p. 75).
Robertson, *Mackintosh at the Hunterian,* p. 46 (illus. pl. 47).

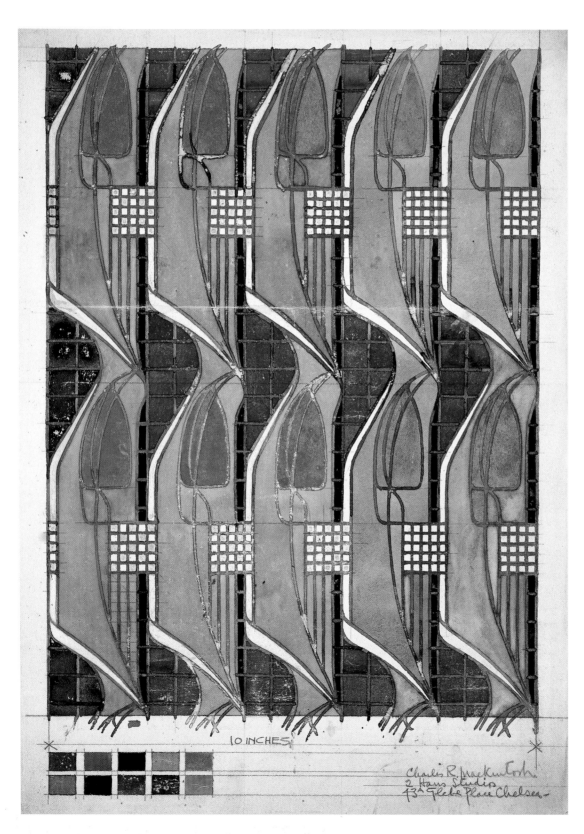

87
Charles Rennie Mackintosh
(designer)

Poster for **The Scottish Musical
Review**
1896
colour lithograph
230 x 85.8 cm
signed and dated on the plate
printed by Banks & Co.,
Glasgow

Glasgow Museums and Art Galleries
77.13ar

In 1895-96 Mackintosh, Herbert
MacNair and the Macdonald
sisters produced a series of rather
unconventional posters. A
combination of human and
organic forms would certainly
have attracted the attention - if
not the approbation - of the
Glasgow public. This design is
dominated by an elongated
human form blocked out in green
against a dark blue background.
The same year Mackintosh used
identical 'oriental' facial features
in a smaller poster (cat. 88) for
the *Scottish Musical Review*. This
figure also has an ambiguous
'organic' quality: a series of
'stems' rise and branch out from
the foot of the design, then flow
into two motifs on either side of
the central figure. The entire
design is brought into focus by
the circular ring or 'moon'
against which the figure is
silhouetted. These two
uppermost motifs clearly relate to
the ironwork finials Mackintosh
used outside the Glasgow School
of Art - likewise in 1896. The
interplay of exaggerated human
and plant-like forms preoccupied
him during this period. Working
in two dimensions, he used
blocks of colour and dense linear
patterns to enhance the
ambiguity.

Exhibitions
1990   Glasgow

The Glasgow Style

88
Charles Rennie Mackintosh
(designer)

Poster for **The Scottish Musical Review**
1896
colour lithograph
53.3 x 40 cm
signed and dated on the plate

Glasgow Museums and Art Galleries
77.13as

Mackintosh used two symmetrical 'singing' birds as a musical motif on several occasions. The organ he designed in 1897 at Glasgow's Craigie Hall incorporated two carved wooden birds in a similar arrangement. He subsequently repeated this detail in his design for the piano in the *House for an Art Lover* (1901: see fig. 3.13, p. 111), just as he reiterated the stylised thistles in the decoration of Craigie Hall, but the thistles figured rarely in his later work. The symbolic meaning and uncompromising boldness of the present design evokes Mackintosh's growing self-confidence and independence during this period.

Exhibitions
1985-86 *Charles Rennie Mackintosh,*
    Tokyo and tour

Literature
Thomas Howarth, *Charles Rennie Mackintosh and the Modern Movement,* London 1990, pp. 27 - 30.

89
Charles Rennie Mackintosh
(designer)

Chair for the Ingram Street Tea Rooms
designed 1900
oak stained dark
151 x 47.3 x 43.3 cm

Glasgow Museums and Art Galleries
E1982.44

Three versions of this design were executed for Miss Cranston's Ingram Street tea rooms from 1900. The construction of the chairs was identical; only their height differed. One version of conventional proportions was used in both the main dining room and the Cloister Room. The elegance of this high-backed example was achieved at the expense of stability and strength. The fact that the two backsplats were not originally attached to the seat rail weakened the chair and rendered it impractical for the constant wear and tear of the tea room. Few examples were actually produced, nor is it clear for which rooms they were intended. Strategically deployed in various locations, their primary purpose may have been aesthetic. Mackintosh kept one example for himself, and had it painted white for his Main Street flat.

Exhibitions
1952   *Victorian and Edwardian Decorative Arts,* Victoria & Albert Museum, London
1953   *Charles Rennie Mackintosh,* Saltire Society and ACGB, Edinburgh (B10)
1960-61 *Sources of the Twentieth Century,* Musée National d'Art Moderne, Paris
1979   *Homespun to Highspeed,* Sheffield City Art Gallery
1983   Turin

Literature
Some examples of furniture by Charles Rennie Mackintosh, Glasgow School of Art, Glasgow 1968 (7)
Robert Macleod, *Charles Rennie Mackintosh,* London 1968 (illus. pl. 77).
Filippo Alison, *Charles Rennie Mackintosh as a Designer of Chairs,* London 1974, pp. 40, 42 - 43, 91 - 95.
Billcliffe, *Mackintosh Furniture and Interiors,* p. 90 (1900.55).

90
Charles Rennie Mackintosh
(designer)

Serving table for the White Dining Room, Ingram Street Tea Rooms
1900
oak painted white
76.8 x 47.2 x 31.2 cm

Glasgow Museums and Art Galleries
E1982.59

Though the main dining area of the Ingram Street tea rooms was painted white, virtually all the furniture was left natural or stained dark. One exception was this serving table, a relatively sturdy piece that, placed next to a table, made it easier to unload tea trays. Mackintosh pierced the table with rectangles (thus reducing its weight) and incised it with squares so that it would match the backs of the dining chairs in the same room (89).

Exhibitions
1979   *Homespun to Highspeed,* Sheffield City Art Gallery
1983   Turin
1986-87 *The Pursuit of Perfection,* touring exhibition

Literature
Billcliffe, *Mackintosh Furniture and Interiors,* p. 91 (1900.6)

91

Charles Rennie Mackintosh
(designer)

Mirror for the Ladies' Dressing Room, Ingram Street Tea Rooms
1900
oak stained green
197 x 60 x 11 cm

Glasgow Museums and Art Galleries
E1982.61

Mackintosh's design for the Ladies' Dressing Room was his first involvement with Miss Cranston's Ingram Street Tea Rooms from 1900. Located off the main dining room on the ground floor, it was probably also painted white. This full-length mirror was fitted into the panelling at the south end of the room. Though the design is simpler, the tapering columns and detailing at the top resemble a cheval mirror Mackintosh designed for the main bedroom at Windyhill, Kilmacolm, the following year. Stained green (as shown) originally, the mirror was probably painted white at some stage. The simplicity of the design is even more apparent when it is compared with the sophisticated, freestanding mirror Mackintosh made for his own Main Street flat in 1900, which was shown that autumn in Vienna (see fig. 3.12, p. 110).

Literature
Billcliffe, *Mackintosh Furniture and Interiors*, p. 93.

92

Charles Rennie Mackintosh
(designer)

Chair for the Hill House, Helensburgh
c. 1904
ebonised wood
111 x 40.6 x 42 cm

Glasgow Museums and Art Galleries
40.16a

The original commission for the Hill House included only a limited amount of new furniture, which Mackintosh started designing in the autumn of 1903. The following year additional pieces were apparently authorised, including a writing desk for the owner of the house, Walter Blackie, and this matching chair. Desk and chair received the same ebonised finish, with the cabinet's geometric decoration echoed by the lattice work of the central backsplat of the chair. The extension of the splats below the level of the seat recalls the chair with a high back that Mackintosh designed for the main bedroom the previous year. Similar lattice detailing recurs in his designs for the interior of Miss Cranston's house at Nitshill during the same period. Mackintosh was obviously pleased with the desk and chair since he replicated them for his own use.

Exhibitions
1933   *Mackintosh Memorial Exhibition*, McLellan Galleries, Glasgow (not in catalogue)
1968   *Charles Rennie Mackintosh, Architecture, Design & Painting*, Edinburgh and tour
1976-77 *Ein Dokument Deutscher Kunst, 1901-76*, Darmstadt
1982   *Charles Rennie Mackintosh*, Kunstindustrimuseum, Copenhagen
1985-86 *Charles Rennie Mackintosh*, Tokyo and tour

Literature
Filippo Alison, *Charles Rennie Mackintosh as a Designer of Chairs*, London 1974, pp. 70 - 71, 100.
Billcliffe, *Mackintosh Furniture and Interiors*, pp. 156 - 157 (1904.17).

93
Charles Rennie Mackintosh
(designer)

*Pay-box for the Chinese Room,
Ingram Street Tea Rooms*
1911
wood painted blue
236.5 x 73 x 102 cm

*Glasgow Museums and Art Galleries
E1982.60*

The Chinese Room was a
refurbishment of an existing
interior by Mackintosh in 1911.
The space was redefined by
means of a series of painted
lattice-work timber screens.
Those around the perimeter of
the room were backed with
painted grass matting or were
used to define concave niches
filled with mirrored glass or
strips of coloured casein-based
plastic. The space was further
divided by free-standing lattice
screens that supported the lattice-
work ceiling. This manipulation
of solid and void was carried
through to the design of the pay-
box. Described by a former
cashier as 'a fantastic cage', it was
set at one end of the room where
it served a semi-structural
purpose by supporting the
lattice-work ceiling. The carved
detail in the canopy corresponds
to a larger carved panel above the
entrance to the room; it, too, was
incorporated in the front and side
rails of the small chairs with
which the room is furnished.

Exhibitions
1968   *Charles Rennie Mackintosh:
         Architecture, Design and
         Painting,* Edinburgh and tour
1984   Glasgow (103)
1990   Glasgow

Literature
Billcliffe, *Mackintosh Furniture and
Interiors,* p. 215 (1911.3).
Anthony Jones, *Charles Rennie
Mackintosh,* London 1990, p. 181.

94
Charles Rennie Mackintosh
(designer)

*Chair for the Chinese Room,
Ingram Street Tea Rooms*
1911
ebonised pine
82.4 x 43.8 x 40.7 cm

*Glasgow Museums and Art Galleries
E1982.45.7*

A total of thirty-six examples of
this chair were listed as
furnishings of the Chinese Room
at the Ingram Street Tea Rooms.
Mackintosh tied them in with the
rest of the interior by repeating
the Chinese-style detailing in the
fretted back, front and side rails
of the chairs. There is no
evidence of any plans to adapt
them to the bold blues and reds
that dominated the room, though
the words '2d extra if enamelled'
in a quotation suggests this may
have been in Mackintosh's mind
at some point.

Exhibitions
1968   *Charles Rennie Mackintosh:
          Architecture, Design and
          Painting,* Edinburgh and tour
1984   Glasgow (103)
1985-86 *Charles Rennie Mackintosh,*
          Tokyo and tour

Literature
Douglas Percy Bliss, *Charles Rennie
Mackintosh and the Glasgow School of
Art,* Glasgow 1961.
Robert Macleod, *Charles Rennie
Mackintosh,* London 1968 (pl. 102).
Filippo Alison, *Charles Rennie
Mackintosh as a Designer of Chairs,*
London 1974, pp. 74 - 75.
Billcliffe, *Mackintosh Furniture and
Interiors,* p. 215 (1911.4).

95
Charles Rennie Mackintosh
(designer)

*Domino table for the Ingram
Street Tea Rooms*
1911
ebonised oak
77.5 x 50 x 50 cm

*Glasgow Museums and Art Galleries
E1982.55*

Mackintosh had designed a
forerunner of this domino table
some fourteen years earlier for
Miss Cranston's Argyle Street
Tea Rooms. Surviving examples
were presumably transferred to
Ingram Street upon its closure in
1920. We cannot be certain
whether this later example was
intended for the Chinese Room,
though its ebonised finish and
certain aspects of its construction
do correspond to the chairs that
furnished the room. Its design,
which is sparer and more
compact than that of the earlier
Argyle Street example, effectively
plays the four quadrant shelves
off against the circular table top.

Exhibitions
1984 Glasgow (103)

Literature
Glasgow School of Art, *Some examples of
furniture by Charles Rennie Mackintosh
in the Glasgow School of Art Collection,*
Glasgow 1968, no. 12.
Robert Macleod, *Charles Rennie
Mackintosh,* London 1968.
Billcliffe, *Mackintosh Furniture and
Interiors,* p. 215 (1911.5).
Anthony Jones, *Charles Rennie
Mackintosh,* London 1990, p. 181.

**Margaret Macdonald
Mackintosh**

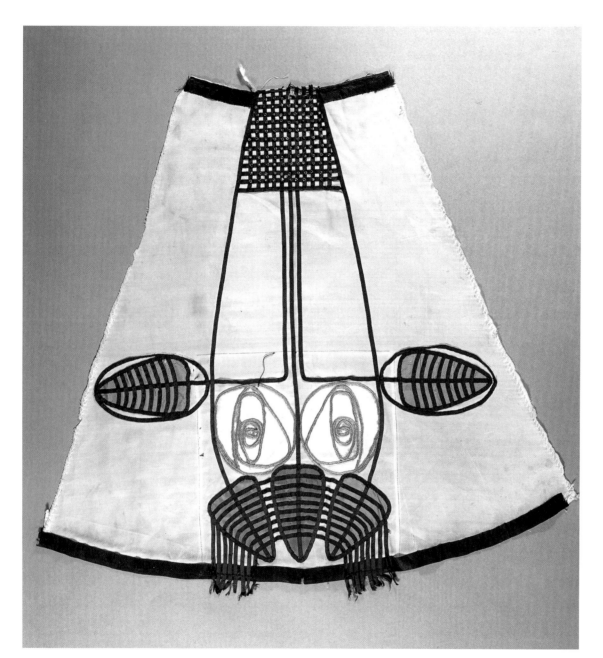

Lampshade panel
1905
white silk with an appliqué
design representing two stylised
roses and five leaves; the design is
made of green and pink silk,
green silk braid and black silk
ribbons with clear glass beads;
the beads along the lower edge
are missing
41.9 x 47 cm

*Glasgow Museums and Art Galleries
E1953.94*

Executed according to a design
by Charles Rennie Mackintosh,
this is one of four lampshade
panels from the standard lamp
made for the drawing room, Hill
House, Helensburgh. Another
panel from the same lampshade is
in the Victoria & Albert
Museum, London.

Collections
Mary Newbery Sturrock

Exhibitions
1980 Glasgow (70)
1983 Turin
1984 Glasgow (52)
1990 Glasgow (228)

Literature
Mary Newbery Sturrock, 'Remembering
Charles Rennie Mackintosh', *The
Connoisseur,* August 1973, pp. 280 - 288.
Billcliffe, *Mackintosh Furniture and
Interiors,* p. 181.
Constance Howard, *Twentieth Century
Embroidery in Great Britain to 1939,*
London 1981, p. 61.

97

Herbert MacNair, Margaret Macdonald and Frances Macdonald (designers)

Poster for the Glasgow Institute of the Fine Arts
c. 1896
colour lithograph
218.5 x 87.7 cm
signed on the plate
Printed in four colours by Carter & Pratt, Glasgow

Glasgow Museums and Art Galleries
77.13au

The obvious similarity between this design and a poster Mackintosh also made for *The Scottish Musical Review* in 1896 (cat. 87) suggests how closely The Four collaborated. The dimensions of the two posters are almost the same, just as the central imagery - figures growing out of stylised plant forms - is very similar. Here the treatment of the two figures is somewhat less abstract, but they are elongated in the same distinctive manner. The poster is rigorously symmetrical and subdivided by strong horizontal lines. The outstretched arms of the male figure clasp a stem from the two rose trees, thus drawing the sides of the design inward, creating tension and strengthening the framework of the central motif, namely the opening flower held by the female figure. The focus is further clarified by the downward gaze of the two figures and the arched bird-in-flight motifs at the top.

Exhibitions
1990   Glasgow

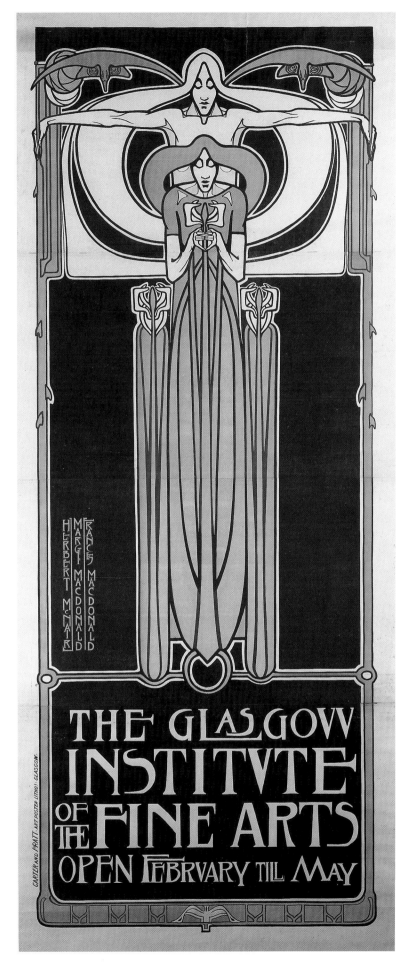

98
Talwin Morris

Christmas card
1897
gouache stencilled on card
26.9 x 18.9 cm (open)

Glasgow Museums and Art Galleries
77.13x

99 a, b
Talwin Morris

Pair of blinds
c. 1900
linen with stencilled decoration
191.5 x 57 cm each

Glasgow Museums and Art Galleries
77.13 an and 77.13 ap

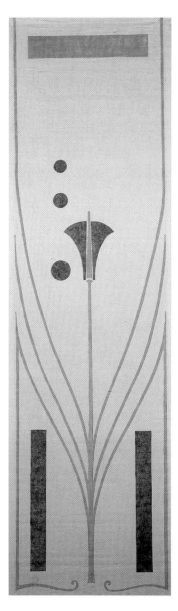

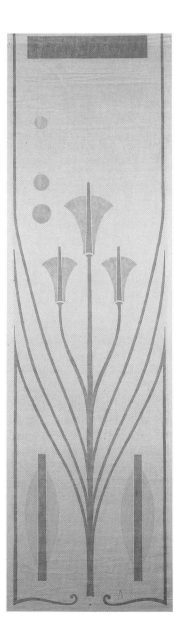

There are no conventional Christmas motifs in this Christmas card from Mr and Mrs Talwin Morris. It is a typically abstracted design in which the human form serves only as a point of departure for Morris's design. The outside of the card is decorated with a single circular motif in green in the top right corner, that has something of the same totemic quality as other motifs designed by The Four during the same period. Its restraint design. contrasts markedly with the colour exuberance of the inside

101
Talwin Morris

Design for decoration of a dining room
1901
watercolour and ink on paper
38 x 57.1 cm

inscribed *'For Mrs Bruno Schroeder/Talwin Morris/ Bowling N.B./Feb 1901'*

Glasgow Museums and Art Galleries 77.13q

100
Talwin Morris

Mirror
c.1900-01
mirrored glass, in a repoussé metal frame set with cabochon 'stones'
56 x 35.6 cm

Glasgow Museums and Art Galleries 46.5g

At the Turin International Exhibition of Decorative Art in 1902 this mirror was priced at five guineas. Several orders for copies are known to have been placed by visitors to the exhibition, but their present whereabouts are unknown.

Exhibitions
1902   Turin

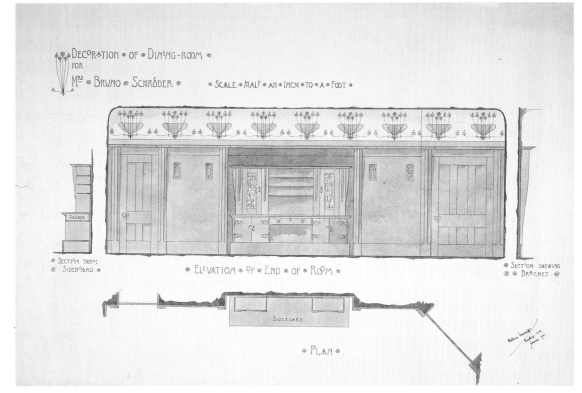

The design illustrates the plan, section and elevation of the end wall of the dining room. The incorporation of a large sideboard flush with the tall, dark panelling is reminiscent of the dining room Mackintosh designed as part of his *House for an Art Lover* competition entry, also in 1901. Here the sideboard is free-standing within what may have been a previously existing recess, rather than built into the panelling itself. The detailing and proportions of the glazed cupboards on either side of the central shelves are characteristic of Morris's furniture. Mackintosh used the flattened heart motif common to the Glasgow Style (and to George Walton and Morris in particular) on several occasions; here it appears as the principal element in the stencilled design above the panelling and in the elaborate door furniture. Mrs Bruno Schroeder has not been identified.

102
Jessie Newbery

Belt
late 1890s
blue linen embroidered with silk
threads in grey, fawn and pale
blue, using straight stitch, French
knots, couching and needle-
weaving; decorated with eight
circular milky glass beads and
fastened with a Russian metal
clasp
5.3 x 66.3 cm

Glasgow Museums and Art Galleries
E1953.53a

Collections
Mary Newbery Sturrock

Exhibitions
1980   Glasgow (110)
1984   Glasgow (25)

103
Jessie Newbery

Collar
early 1900s
deep rose-coloured velvet with
pink silk thread in two
thicknesses and appliqué
rectangles of dark grey velvet
bearing semi-circular and pear-
shaped glass beads in two shades
of green: worked in buttonhole
stitch, French knots and
couching, and fastened with a
Russian metal clasp
overall width 60.9 cm
back neck to hem 21.5 cm

Glasgow Museums and Art Galleries
E1953.53b

The design incorporates
buttonholes around the edge of
the neck for securing the collar to
buttons on the neck of the dress.
These functional buttons formed
an integral part of the design. The
collar was made for Newbery's
daughter, Mary.

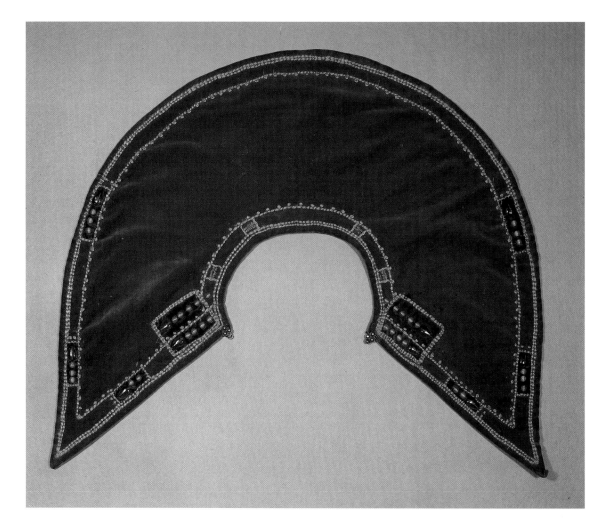

Collections
Mary Newbery Sturrock

Exhibitions
1980   Glasgow (94)
1984   Glasgow(129)

Literature
Margaret Swain, 'Mrs Newbery's Dress',
Costume 12 (1978), pp. 64 - 73.
Constance Howard, *Twentieth Century*
Embroidery in Great Britain to 1939,
London 1981, p. 61.
Burkhauser, *Glasgow Girls,* pp. 146 - 147
(illus. fig. 191, inset).

Collar
c. 1905
blue velvet embroidered with two
thicknesses of grey silk threads
using satin stitch, French knots

104
Jessie Newbery

Cushion cover
1899-1900
unbleached linen embroidered
with crewel wools in two shades
of blue and green, three shades of
pink and white, fawn and yellow,
using long, short and stem
stitches with a border of needle-
weaving
55.8 x 48.8 cm
inscribed *'Under every/ grief and
pine/runs a joy/with silken twine'*

*Glasgow Museums and Art Galleries
1953.53c*

The inscription, from a poem by
William Blake, is surrounded by
stylised pea pods and flowers.
The fastening has been
emphasised by means of blue
woollen lacing ending in tassels.
Jessie Newbery often practised
needle-weaving, a technique she
first saw used by Italian needle-
workers on a visit to that country
in 1882. A matching curtain was
illustrated in *The Studio* in 1900,
but its present whereabouts are
unknown.

Collections
Mary Newbery Sturrock

Exhibitions
1980   Glasgow (92)
1982   Glasgow (77)
1984   Glasgow (124)
1990   Glasgow (216)

Literature
The Studio 19 (1900), p. 235.
Liz Arthur, 'Glasgow School of Art
Embroidery 1894-1920', *The Journal of
the Decorative Arts Society* 4, pp. 18 - 25.
Constance Howard, *Twentieth Century
Embroidery in Great Britain to 1939*,
London 1981, p. 48.
Margaret Swain, *Scottish Embroidery -
Medieval to Modern*, London 1986 p. 141
(illus.).
Burkhauser, *Glasgow Girls*, p. 149 (illus.
fig. 194).

and couching; decorated with
semi-circular ivory coloured
beads and flat oval mother-of-
pearl discs; fastened with a
Russian metal clasp
overall width 62.5 cm
back neck to hem 24 cm

*Glasgow Museums and Art Galleries
E1985.162.1*

Newbery made the collar for her
daughter, Mary.

Collections
Mary Newbery Sturrock

Exhibitions
1980   Glasgow (106)

Literature
Margaret Swain, 'Mrs. J.R. Newbery
(1864-1948)', *Embroidery* 24 (1973), p.
106.
Burkhauser, *Glasgow Girls*, p. 146 (illus.
fig. 191, inset).

106
Margaret Swanson and Ann Macbeth

Educational Needlework
Published by Longmans,
London 1911

Glasgow Museums and Art Galleries

This book introduced a new method of teaching children needlework which took into account their developing hand and eye co-ordination. It described a number of projects for children of various ages and emphasised that they should be introduced to colour at an early age and learn gradually with the guidance of a well trained, understanding teacher. The scheme roused widespread interest and was quickly adopted. Specimens of the work described in the book were requested by schools in Britain, Africa, America, the West Indies and India. The method was used in Scottish schools until the 1960s.

107
Ernest Archibald Taylor

Design for a glazed cabinet
c. 1900
pencil and watercolour on paper
19.5 x 15 cm

Glasgow Museums and Art Galleries
E1982.77.1

The control and delicate economy of Taylor's design demonstrates his ability as a draughtsman. An inscription at the bottom of the drawing states that the piece was executed by Wylie & Lochhead Ltd. The drawing may have been produced retrospectively, as a record of the completed piece. The design is composed of a series of elements repeatedly found in his furniture from about 1900: the pronounced overhanging cornice, the pierced gables, the circular drop handles, the stained glass panels and the curved and incised aprons are all part of his design vocabulary.

Exhibitions
1983   *Some Glasgow Style Designers*,
         Glasgow Museums and Art
         Galleries

Ernest Archibald Taylor

Glasgow Museums and Art Galleries
E1982.77.2

Design for oak dining-room
furniture
c. 1899-1900
pencil, ink and watercolour on
paper

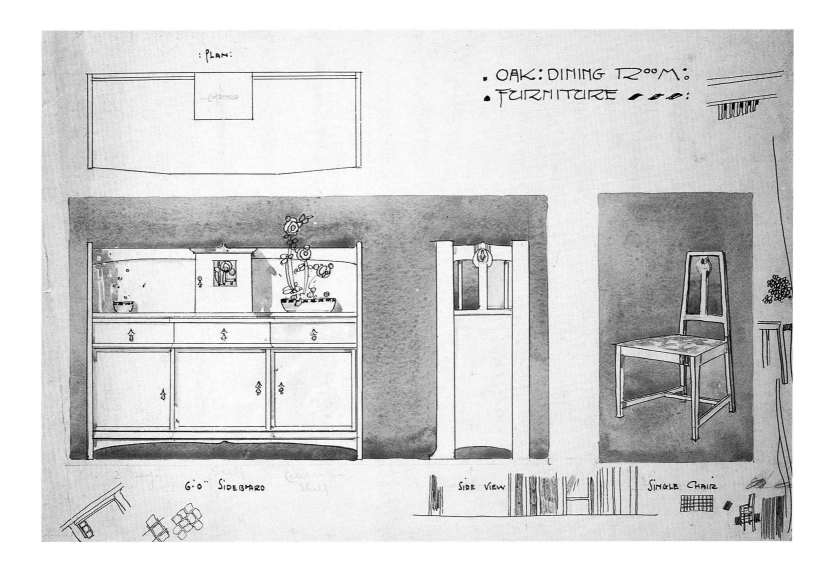

The ink 'doodles' round the edge of the design indicate that the sheet derives from Taylor's sketchbook. It is not as carefully finished as other surviving examples of his furniture drawings, which constitute the less decorative side of Taylor's output. The sideboard incorporates only one stained glass panel, located on the central cupboard; there are other decorations, such as the small detail at the centre of the gable, but the overall effect is simple and restrained. A pencilled inscription beneath each of the three cupboard doors specifies its function: the inscription on the left reads '2 Trays', in the centre 'Shelf' and on the right 'Celerette Shelf'. The chair is equally uncomplicated, with only a hint of decoration on the central backsplat.

Exhibitions
1983   *Some Glasgow Style Designers*,
        Glasgow Museums and Art
        Galleries

109
Ernest Archibald Taylor

Design for mantel and fireplace
c. 1900
ink, watercolour, body colour
and silver paint on paper
26.8 x 25.6 cm

Glasgow Museums and Art Galleries
E1982.77.3

Some of the most striking
examples of the Glasgow Style
are designs for fireplaces. The
present design shows how Taylor
exploited the opportunities they
afforded for using different
materials and decorating the
mantel. The coloured washes and
silver paint suggest the variety of
materials he planned to employ.
The pair of stained-glass
cupboard doors in the centre of
the mantel are flanked by two
single smaller ones. The mantel
itself is supported by an
elaborately carved surround.
According to a note at the
bottom of the drawing, the piece
was to have been finished in
white enamel. Though another
inscription states that it was
executed by Wylie & Lochhead,
the building for which it was
intended has not been identified.

110
Ernest Archibald Taylor
(designer)

Display cabinet
1901
maple
189.5 x 139 x 38 cm

Glasgow Museums and Art Galleries
E1981.126

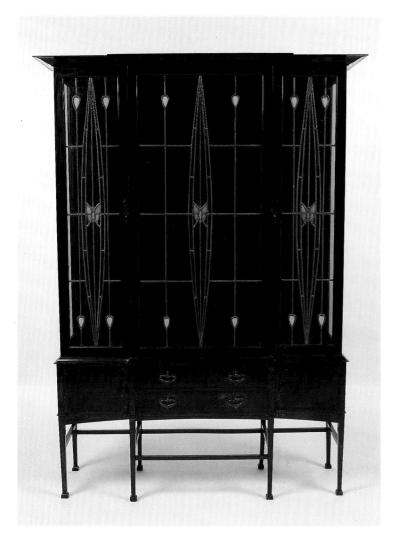

111
Ernest Archibald Taylor
(designer)

Chair
1901
walnut with satinwood and
mother-of-pearl inlay
modern upholstery
83.5 x 43 x 45.5 cm

Glasgow Museums and Art Galleries
E1991.29.1

Collections
Purchased by an employee of Wylie &
Lochhead, and bequeathed to his
nephew, Mr Fraser; purchased from Mr
Fraser's widow through Bourne Fine
Art, Edinburgh, in 1981

Exhibitions
1901   Glasgow International
        Exhibition
1902   *Exhibition of British Arts and
        Crafts,* National Museum of
        Applied Arts, Budapest
1984   Glasgow (145)
1985   *Glasgow-Budapest 1902,*
        Glasgow Museums and Art
        Galleries
According to a descendant of the
cabinet's first owner, it was also exhibited
in London.

Literature
The Art Journal (1901), pp. 241 and 300.
The Studio 23 (1901), pp. 166 - 167.
Wylie & Lochhead Souvenir booklet,
1901, p. 17.
The Journal of Decorative Art, July 1901,
p. 180.
The Exhibition Illustrated, 20 July 1901,
p. 247.
The Studio 33 (1904), pp. 219 - 222.
Wylie & Lochhead furnishing catalogue,
c. 1905 (with the National Art Library,
London).
Gerald and Celia Larner, *The Glasgow
Style,* Edinburgh 1979, p. 64.
Juliet Kinchin, 'The Wylie & Lochhead
Style', *The Journal of the Decorative Arts
Society* 9 (1985), pp. 4 - 16.

Together with an armchair
version, examples of this design
were exhibited as part of the
furnishings in the drawing room
of Wylie & Lochhead's pavilion
at the Glasgow International
Exhibition of 1901 (see fig. 3.10,
p. 108). Its construction is almost
identical to that of a chair Taylor
subsequently made for the
drawing room of 32 Radnor
Road in Birmingham, a large
commission that he received as a
direct result of the Glasgow
Exhibition. The inlaid mother-of-
pearl butterflies on the backsplat
recall the central motif of
Taylor's drawing room scheme,
and set this piece apart from the
more conservative decoration he
used in Birmingham. After being
exhibited in Budapest in 1902,
one of the armchairs was
acquired by that city's
Iparmüvészeti Collection.

Exhibitions
1901   Glasgow International
        Exhibition
1902   *Exhibition of British Arts and
        Crafts,* National Museum of
        Applied Arts, Budapest

E.A. Taylor worked closely with
the Glasgow firm of furniture
makers Wylie & Lochhead. In
1901 he was charged with
designing the drawing room in
their pavilion at the Glasgow
Exhibition (fig. 3.10). The
exhibited cabinet was presumably
built for this particular interior,
though more than one version of
it could well have been made.
Contemporary descriptions
indicate that it was stained grey
and that details were highlighted
with violet and green stains so
that the piece would match the
'lightness and grace' of Taylor's
colour scheme. The large
overhanging cornice, the heart-
shaped drawer handles and, in
particular, the butterfly motif in
the leaded glass panels are all part
of Taylor's design vocabulary,
and characteristic features of the
Glasgow Style.

112
George Walton (designer)

Armchair
1900
oak with modern upholstery
104 x 48.2 x 43.5 cm

Glasgow Museums and Art Galleries
E1981.125.4

This armchair originally belonged to a dining room suite that in turn formed part of a larger domestic commission completed in late 1900 for Sydney Paterson of Bickley, Kent. A sketch of the chair appears in Walton's ledger of furniture designs entitled 'The Brussels Long Back Chair' - a reference to the showroom he designed and furnished for the Kodak Photographic Company at 59 Montagne de la Cour, Brussels. By the time the showroom opened in September 1901, versions of the chair had already begun to appear in Walton's domestic work. Examples were also exhibited at the Glasgow International Exhibition from May 1901. This was not the only time Walton used the same design with little or no modification for both domestic and commercial commissions. The small heart shape incised in the backsplat discreetly signals the introduction of a motif that dominated Walton's Glasgow-based work. It is a quiet reminder of his Glasgow roots within the context of a design that demonstrates Walton's growing preoccupation with eighteenth-century models, following his departure for London in 1897. He retained at least two examples of the design for his own use.

Exhibitions
1901   Glasgow International Exhibition
1902   *Exhibition of British Arts and Crafts,* National Museum of Applied Arts, Budapest
1984   Glasgow (16)

Literature
Dekorative Kunst 8 (1901), p. 492.
The Kodak Properties, Eastman Kodak Company, London 1906.
The Studio Yearbook 1907, p. 96.

113
George Walton (designer)

The 'Lovat' toilet table
1900
walnut with stencilled linen hangings and mirror
179 x 171 x 43.5 cm

Glasgow Museums and Art Galleries
E1982.38

Walton designed the 'Lovat' line of furniture between 1899 and about 1901. Consisting of at least seven different furniture types, it appears to have evolved in the course of several different commissions, starting with the decoration and furnishing of the Elm Bank in York in 1898. The line included a wash-stand that was exhibited alongside the toilet table in the 'bedroom' of Walton's stand at the 1901 Glasgow International Exhibition. The piece exemplifies his work at the turn of the century, particularly with respect to the pronounced cabriole front legs and the small hearts incised above each mirror. The deer-and-leaf design on the two linen hangings is a simplification of the stencil Walton used in the billiard room of the Argyle Street Tea Rooms, Glasgow, in 1897. A similar pattern was also used for a wallpaper introduced by Jeffrey and Co. in 1904.

Exhibitions
1901   Glasgow International Exhibition
1984   Glasgow (not in catalogue)
1989   *Ten Years of The Fine Art Society in Glasgow,* The Fine Art Society, Glasgow
1990   *Scotland Creates: 5000 Years of Art and Design,* McLellan Galleries, Glasgow (G20)

Literature
Dekorative Kunst 8 (1901), p. 492.
W. Shaw Sparrow, *British Homes of Today,* London 1904, fig. D11.
The Studio Year Book 1907, p. 96.
Roger Billcliffe, 'How many Swallows make a Summer? Art and Design in Glasgow in 1900', *Scotland Creates: 5000 Years of Art and Design,* London 1990, p. 145 (illus. 9.15).

114
Helen Walton (possibly
together with Hannah Walton)

Part of a Water Set
c. 1910

(a) jug
height 14.7 cm
base diameter 11 cm

(b) tumbler
height 11 cm
base diameter 5.5 cm

(c) finger bowl
height 6 cm
diameter 10.4 cm

(d) finger bowl
height 5 cm
diameter 11.3 cm
all clear glass with enamel
decoration

Glasgow Museums and Art Galleries
E1989.7.1.3.5 and 14

In the early twentieth century interest in enamel decoration revived not only in France and Central Europe, but also in Britain, and especially Scotland, albeit to a lesser extent. Many graduates of the Glasgow School of Art decorated plain commercial ceramic and glassware, and the Walton sisters more than anyone else. Since they sometimes worked together and sometimes alone, and did not sign everything they made, it is often difficult to distinguish their work. Most of it they gave to friends and acquaintances as gifts. The intended purpose of their wares is indicated by the decorative motifs on them - usually plants, animals or mythological creatures associated with water.

The glass itself cannot be traced to any Scottish manufacturer of the period, but may have been produced by Powell's of Whitefriars, London, since the sisters' brother George sold their products in his Glasgow shop.

115
Marion Wilson

Triptych
c. 1905
beaten tin
centre panel 59 x 60.2 cm
side panels each 59 x 27 cm
signed

Glasgow Museums and Art Galleries
E1984.46a, b, c

116
Ellison Young
Tablecloth
1907
natural linen with a green linen
border: worked in three shades of
green, two shades of purple and
white floss silk threads in satin

The rose, either in the form of a
single stylised bloom or as part of
a standard tree form, was
commonly used as a decorative
motif by several exponents of the
Glasgow Style. It was even
chosen as the principal theme of
the Rose Boudoir room setting at
the Turin Exhibition of 1902.
Roses were used to decorate
furniture, embroideries, stained
glass and metalwork. The
multiplicity of symbolic
meanings assigned to the flower -
from purity to burning passion,
from Venus to the Virgin Mary -
suited it pre-eminently to the
needs of such secretive religious
societies as the Rosicrucians.
The two side panels support
mirror images of a rose, while in
the central panel a young woman
contemplates a rose within a
stylised geometric bower.

Exhibitions
1984   Glasgow (175)
1990   Glasgow

Literature
Burkhauser, *Glasgow Girls*, pp. 105 - 106
(illus. fig. 134).

and straight stitches with a
cutwork and needle-woven
border, inscribed '*Friendship is a
sheltering tree, Flowers are lovely,
Love is Flower like*'.
116.7 x 116.7 cm

Glasgow Museums and Art Galleries
E1980.169.6

Collections
Miss H. Maitland

Exhibitions
1984   Glasgow (181)

Select bibliography

Industry and art

Auld, Alasdair *et al.*
*Glasgow Art Gallery and Museum:
The Building and the Collection*, Glasgow
(Collins / Glasgow Museums and Art
Galleries) 1987

Checkland, Sydney
'Scottish Urban Life at the Turn of the
Century', *Art, Design and the Quality of Life
in Turn of the Century Scotland 1890-1910*,
Dundee (Duncan of Jordanstone College of
Art) 1983, pp. 1 - 24

Checkland, Olive and Sydney
Industry and Ethos: Scotland 1832-1914,
Edinburgh (Edinburgh University Press) 1989

Cooper, Douglas (intro.)
Alex Reid & Lefèvre 1926-1976, London
(Lefèvre Gallery) 1976

De Leeuw, Ronald, John Sillevis, Charles
Dumas (eds.)
*The Hague School: Dutch Masters of the 19th
Century*, London (Weidenfeld and Nicolson)
1983

*French Paintings and Drawings: Illustrated
Summary Catalogue*, Glasgow (Art Gallery
and Museum) 1985

Fowle, Frances
'The Hague School and the Scots: a Taste for
Dutch Pictures', *Apollo* (August 1991),
pp. 108 - 111

Gould, B.
*Two Van Gogh Contacts: E.J. Van Wisselingh,
Art Dealer; Daniel Cottier, Glass Painter and
Decorator*, London (Naples Press) 1969

Gomme, Andor and David Walker
Architecture of Glasgow, London (Lund
Humphries) 1987

Kaplan, Wendy (ed.)
*Scotland Creates: 5000 Years of Art and
Design*, London (Weidenfeld and Nicolson)
1990

Lloyd Williams, Julia *et al.*
Dutch Art and Scotland: A Reflection of Taste,
Edinburgh (National Galleries of Scotland)
1992

Marks, Richard
Burrell. Portrait of a Collector, Glasgow
(Richard Drew Publishing) 1983

Pickvance, Ronald
A Man of Influence: Alex Reid 1854-1928,
Edinburgh (Scottish Arts Council) 1968

Williamson, Elizabeth, Anne Riches, Malcolm
Higgs, *Buildings of Scotland: Glasgow*,
London (Penguin) 1990

The Glasgow School of Painters

Billcliffe, Roger
Mackintosh Watercolours, London (John Murray) 1978

Billcliffe, Roger
Sir James Guthrie and the Scottish Realists, Glasgow (The Fine Art Society) 1981

Billcliffe, Roger
The Glasgow Boys, London (John Murray) 1985; repr. 1990

Billcliffe, Roger
Edward Atkinson Hornel 1864-1933, Glasgow (The Fine Art Society) 1983

Brown, David
John Quinton Pringle, Edinburgh (Scottish Arts Council) 1981

Buchanan, William (ed.)
The Glasgow Boys, 2 vols., Edinburgh (Scottish Arts Council) 1968 and 1971

Buchanan, William
Mr Henry and Mr Hornel Visit Japan, Edinburgh (Scottish Arts Council) 1978

Deslandes, Gerald
Arthur Melville 1855-1904, Dundee (Dundee Museums and Art Galleries) 1977

Hamilton, Vivien
Joseph Crawhall 1861-1913: One of the Glasgow Boys, London (John Murray) 1990

Hardie, William
Scottish Painting 1837 to the Present, London (Cassell) 1990

McConkey, Kenneth
'From Grez to Glasgow: French Naturalist Influence in Scottish Painting', *The Scottish Art Review* 15, no. 4 (1982), pp. 16 - 34

McConkey, Kenneth
Sir John Lavery RA 1856-1941, Belfast and London (Ulster Museum and The Fine Art Society) 1984

Mackay, Agnes E.
Arthur Melville: Scottish Impressionist, Leigh-on-Sea 1951

Macmillan, Duncan
Scottish Art 1460-1990, Edinburgh (Mainstream) 1990

Martin, David
The Glasgow School of Painting, London (George Bell & Sons) 1897; repr. Edinburgh (Paul Harris) 1976

Robertson, Pamela
Mackintosh Flower Drawings, Glasgow (Hunterian Art Gallery) 1988

The Scottish Art Review, Glasgow 1888-89

The Scottish Art Review, 2nd series, Glasgow 1946-87

Weller, Helen
E.A. Walton, Edinburgh (Bourne Fine Art) 1981

The Glasgow Style

Alison, Filippo
Charles Rennie Mackintosh as a Designer of Chairs, London 1974

Billcliffe, Roger
Mackintosh Textile Designs, London (John Murray) 1982

Billcliffe, Roger
Mackintosh Furniture, Cambridge (Lutterworth Press) 1984

Billcliffe, Roger
Charles Rennie Mackintosh: The Complete Furniture, Furniture Drawings and Interior Designs, 3rd ed., London (John Murray) 1986

Blench, Brian *et al.*
The Glasgow Style 1890-1920, Glasgow (Glasgow Museums and Art Galleries) 1984

Buchanan, William (ed.)
Mackintosh's Masterwork. The Glasgow School of Art, Glasgow (Richard Drew Publishing) 1989

Burkhauser, Jude *et al.*
Glasgow Girls: Women in the Art School 1880-1920, Glasgow (Glasgow School of Art) 1988

Burkhauser, Jude (ed.)
'Glasgow Girls': Women in Art and Design 1880-1920, Edinburgh (Canongate) 1990

Callen, Anthea
Angel in the Studio: Women in the Arts and Crafts Movement, London (Astragal Books) 1979

Cumming, Elizabeth, and Wendy Kaplan
The Arts and Crafts Movement, London (Thames and Hudson) 1991

Donnelly, Michael
Glasgow Stained Glass: A Preliminary Study, 2nd ed., Glasgow (Glasgow Museums and Art Galleries) 1985

Helland, Janice
The 'New Woman' in Fin-de-Siècle Art: Margaret and Frances Macdonald, unpublished Ph.D. thesis, University of Victoria 1991

Howarth, Thomas
Charles Rennie Mackintosh and the Modern Movement, 2nd ed., London (Routledge and Kegan Paul) 1977; repr. 1990

Kinchin, Juliet
'The Wylie & Lochhead Style', *Journal of the Decorative Arts Society* 9 (1985), pp. 4 - 16

Kinchin, Perilla and Juliet Kinchin
Glasgow's Great Exhibitions: 1888, 1901, 1911, 1938, 1988, Wendlebury (White Cockade Publishing) 1988

Kinchin, Perilla
Tea and Taste: The Glasgow Tea Rooms 1875-1975, Wendlebury (White Cockade Publishing) 1991

Larner, Gerald and Celia
The Glasgow Style, Edinburgh (Paul Harris) 1979

Macfarlane, Fiona C. and Elizabeth F. Arthur
Glasgow School of Art Embroidery 1894-1920, Glasgow (Glasgow Museums and Art Galleries) 1980

Newsletters of the Charles Rennie Mackintosh Society. Glasgow 1978-

Macleod, Robert
Charles Rennie Mackintosh: Artist and Architect, 2nd ed., Feltham 1983

Muthesius, Hermann
The English House, translated from the German by Janet Seligman and edited, with an intro., by Dennis Sharp, London (Crosby Lockwood Staples) 1979; repr. Oxford (BSP Professional Books) 1987

Nuttgens, Patrick (ed.)
Mackintosh and His Contemporaries in Europe and America, London (John Murray) 1988

Parry, Linda
Textiles of the Arts and Crafts Movement, London (Thames and Hudson) 1988

Reekie, Pamela
Margaret Macdonald Mackintosh, Glasgow (Hunterian Art Gallery) 1983

Robertson, Pamela
Charles Rennie Mackintosh: The Chelsea Years, Glasgow (Hunterian Art Gallery) 1987

Robertson, Pamela (ed.)
Charles Rennie Mackintosh. The Architectural Papers, Wendlebury (White Cockade Publishing) in association with the Hunterian Art Gallery, University of Glasgow 1990

Robertson, Pamela
Charles Rennie Mackintosh: The Architectural Drawings, Glasgow (Hunterian Art Gallery) 1990

Robertson, Pamela
Charles Rennie Mackintosh at the Hunterian Art Gallery, Glasgow (Hunterian Art Gallery) 1991

Swain, Margaret
Scottish Embroidery, London (Batsford) 1986

Vergo, Peter
Art in Vienna 1898-1918, 2nd ed., Oxford (Phaidon) 1981

Young, Andrew McLaren
Charles Rennie Mackintosh (1868-1928): Architecture, Design and Painting, Edinburgh (Edinburgh Festival Society) 1968

Colophon

This catalogue is published to coincide with
the exhibition
Glasgow 1900, Art & Design
at the Van Gogh Museum in Amsterdam
from 20 November 1992 to 7 February 1993.

Editors
Elizabeth Cumming, Edinburgh
Andrew McCormick, Amsterdam

General editors
Edwin Becker, Amsterdam
Aly Noordermeer, Amsterdam

General coordination
Stefan van Raay, Amsterdam
Aly Noordermeer, Amsterdam
Hugh Stevenson, Glasgow

Design
Robert Schaap, Bergeyk

Printing
Waanders Printers, Zwolle

Photographs
All photographs have been provided by the
museums or owners of the works unless
otherwise stated. Biographical photos taken
by T. & R. Annan (The Annan Collection,
Glasgow).

© **Copyright 1992**
Uitgeverij Waanders b.v., Zwolle
Van Gogh Museum, Amsterdam

CIP-Gegevens Koninklijke Bibliotheek,
Den Haag

Cumming, E

Glasgow 1900/E. Cumming; red.
A. McCormick.-Zwolle: Waanders.-III.
Uitg. in samenw. met het Van Gogh Museum,
Amsterdam.- Tentoonstellingscatalogus.
ISBN 90 6630 390 5 geb.
ISBN 90 6630 389 1 (museumeditie) pbk.
NUGI 912/921
Trefw.: Glasgow; kunstgeschiedenis